TAKE OFF!

21 HIGH-FLYING SECRETS FOR CAREER SUCCESS

STEPHEN A. FORTE

Cloud Nine
ORLANDO, FLORIDA

To receive three additional career success tools, register directly at
HighFlyingSuccessSecrets.com

Edited by Barb Gam Tagge
Back cover photo by Alis Nikolson
Cover Design by Tanja Prokup
Book Layout ©2019 BookDesignTemplates.com
Printed and distributed by Ingram Spark

Ordering Information:
Quantity sales. Special discounts are available on quantity purchases by corporations, associations, and others. For details, contact the author at web site above.

TAKE OFF! / Stephen A. Forte —1st ed.
ISBN 978-1-7330107-0-2

Contents

Dedication
For my family

Acknowledgments

I would like to extend very special thanks to my editor, Barb Gam Tagge for her creative input, keeping me honest, and encouraging me when I thought I'd never finish this book. Gratitude is also due to novelist Mark Noce for both his frank advice and his invaluable insights into the publishing business; to author Fred Waterman for the constructive criticism I needed to make this book better; Liz Corradino for keeping me out of legal hot water; Craig Forte for his marketing genius; Geary Padden, a real fighter pilot who provided technical expertise; and comedian, writer, director, actor Matt Walsh, who encouraged me to follow my muse and provided some expert comedic advice. I am also grateful to C. V. D. for reminding me of our old high school haunts, especially the castle, his former home. If it weren't for Eddie Robbins being brave enough to fly with me when I was 17, and Dan Wolfe, who hired me to fly the Learjet, I would not have so many stories to share. These people and others enabled me to pursue my dreams and make them a reality.

CHAPTER 1

FROM VISION TO REALITY

> Allow your passion to become your purpose,
> and one day it will become your profession.
>
> —Gabrielle Bernstein

I'm sitting in the captain's seat of a jumbo jet at O'Hare airport, waiting to take off. Instead of quickly departing, we sit.

O'Hare is busy today—it seems always to be, but today airplanes are idling, nose to tail, on every available inch of concrete. It's a hot, sunny, humid fall afternoon, just like the unseasonably sultry day I saw my first airplane when I was a boy.

To my left, I see a four-engine B747-400 jet at the far end of the runway. It is heavy today because it is flying somewhere far away. Several hundred thousand pounds of its total weight are comprised of fuel to make that trip. Like some restless dragon eager to take wing, the plane rests on the runway, engines humming, wings burdened with fuel.

Amid the constant radio chatter piped through my headset, I hear the controller clear the waiting jet to our left for takeoff. Years ago, in a small plane with my father, those words sounded like gibberish. But now the familiar staccato tone sounds confident, even reassuring, and the pilot acknowledges the command in the same calm manner that my father once used.

Small clouds of white smoke billow from each of the four big engines as the pilot adds full power. The air behind the engines ripples from the heat, like the air above a hot desert landscape. The plane starts its takeoff roll, and we barely perceive its motion. It lumbers down the runway toward us, slowly at first. As it approaches it gathers speed, and the massive wings begin to lift. Soon, the radio chatter is briefly drowned out, and all we can hear is the roar of the engines. The wings have risen farther and support more and more of the weight as the plane nears flying speed.

Any time now.

Our eyes follow the plane from left to right, tracking it like a dragster down the long runway. As it passes, we feel the kinetic energy of 875,000 pounds of aluminum, jet fuel, and humanity, and the sound resonates like a buzz in my head. Our stationary position is at a legal distance but still unnervingly close. You don't often see something that big, moving that fast, that close to you.

A moment after it passes, we feel its wake. The mass of air it is pushing out of the way, a gust of man-made wind jolts our airplane.

Near the runway's end, the nose finally rises, but the main wheels are still on the ground. The airplane hesitates, almost as if it is straining, groaning. Then, finally, the other 14 wheels slowly extend from their struts and the colossal machine rises into the air. The wheels dangle for a few moments as the jet gains altitude, and suddenly the belly opens. The big tires are sucked in, and the doors close, leaving a sleek exterior designed solely for flight.

For a fleeting moment, I forget where I am as I watch yet another miracle of flight disappearing into the afternoon sun. The next time those wheels touch down, they will be half a world away.

Although I have done this nearly all my life, it never gets old. When I was a child, it was like an impossible magic trick, and I wanted nothing more than to be the magician. Here I am now, with the sun on my face, the experiences of a lifetime, and still the wonder of a child. What does that say?

After a lifetime of doing the same thing, I am still in love with it. It has always been my passion, so it's also a pleasure. Sure, I have bad days, but the good days make it all worthwhile. You can have a job, or you can find your passion. Here's how I found mine. I hope it helps you find yours.

Chapter 2

TEND TO YOUR DREAMS

The only way to do great work is to love what you do.

—Steve Jobs

It was a cloudless and unusually warm fall afternoon in 1962 at our home in Media, Pennsylvania. I was six years old on our front stoop, counting the ants that marched across the white concrete. My dad had just finished cutting the lawn, and the air was sweet with the smell of freshly cut grass. His damp white T-shirt clung to him with sweat. Our only relief from the relentless heat was the occasional puff of wind and some shade from the broad green leaves of our maple tree.

"Steve, look up!"

He pointed to a dot in the sky that grew bigger and bigger. The dot slowly turned into a single airplane that buzzed straight over our heads and vanished with a whoosh. That was the first airplane I had ever seen.

"That's a military airplane, and those are bombs under his wings," Dad said matter-of-factly.

Maybe because it was a moment shared with my dad, or because I had never seen anything that exciting before, I was bewitched. I had no idea that the cool-looking airplane was the sign of a dire world situation occurring beyond the safety of my backyard.

That month, in October 1962, Russia and the United States were flirting with nuclear war during the Cuban Missile Crisis. Pilots in a U-2 spy plane discovered that the Soviets were building medium-range missile sites in Cuba that could easily hit the East Coast of the United States, including my little community in Pennsylvania. The world faced all-out war as negotiations dragged on for six tense days before reaching a peaceful solution.

I was too young to know it was a bad sign to have that combat aircraft flying over my quiet, suburban neighborhood. I was just intrigued by it. That afternoon and that flyover became a siren's call. I wanted to know how that pilot got there and how he was so lucky to be flying fast and low above us.

The rest of my early aviation memories line up like points plotted on a map to my North Star. The Flying W Airport in Lumberton, New Jersey, sitting on the ramp with my father in a banana-colored Cessna 310. Going to the Philadelphia International Airport and parking at the end of the runway to watch noisy jets smoke low overhead. The jet exhaust and burned rubber smelled like a charcoal barbecue. And, if I close my eyes, I am sitting in the living room of my family home watching my first airline movie with my dad, *The High and the Mighty*. It was a rainy Saturday afternoon, and distant thunder claps occasionally interrupted the dialogue from the tiny speaker in our black-and-white TV. I would take any opportunity to watch a film about flying with my dad. It combined two of the things that have always been the most important to me: flying and family, which consisted of my mom, Marie; my dad, Tony; my sisters, Kathryn and Margie; and my brother, Craig.

My first flight on an airliner was for a family vacation, aboard a big TWA jet. I was going to Arizona, but we may as well have been going to the moon, as excited as I was. I sat by the window over the wing because my dad claimed the ride was better there for my airsick-prone mother. I watched people skittering around the tarmac, loading bags, fueling the plane. The faint smell of kerosene in the cabin that annoyed most passengers smelled like perfume to me.

Finally, we pushed back, taxied out, and took off. I remember annoying my dad and the guy behind me as I repeatedly leaned forward during takeoff, letting the acceleration flop me into the seat.

Throughout the flight, I pressed my nose to the window, watching the many panels moving on the wing, components I would learn to name much later. I was fascinated by the bursts of steam that would appear over the top of the wing as we swooped in and out of the clouds.

After we landed, we visited the cockpit. There were three seats, one each for the captain, first officer, and flight engineer. They were in a cave of metal and glass, surrounded by a sea of tiny round dials and a few levers that were all a mystery to me. I'd never seen an airline pilot before, and this one was like a celebrity, with his shiny gold wings and gleaming gold epaulets. From here they controlled this giant plane. They were human gods, defying gravity.

My next flight was on a smaller jet that had three engines in the plane's tail. While most people would eschew the seat right next to the engine, I requested it. I relished the groan and whine of the big turbofans during every phase of flight, from taxi to take off, cruise to landing. I especially loved the descending moan they made at the end of the flight when the pilot shut them down.

As I grew up, I spent hours staring at the clouds, building my own fleet of model airplanes, and begging my dad to take me to the airport again and again. All that time I longed for the day when I would be the one flying that big silver jet.

I was lucky that my passion literally flew into my life at an early age. I lived, breathed, and tasted aviation. Something is waiting for you, too, if you are open to experiences, pay attention to the moments that have meaning for you, and hold on with both hands.

CHAPTER 3

EMBRACE FAILURE: LIFE'S TEACHABLE MOMENT

Everybody's got a different circle of competence.
The important thing is not how big the circle is.
The important thing is staying inside the circle.

—Warren Buffett

No matter what career or hobby you choose, that commitment will require a continuous cycle of learning. As soon as you think you have mastered one challenging task, move on to the next one. If I have learned one thing in my encounters with people who have successfully pursued their passions, it's that they continuously improve without fail, especially when they fail. The exception is professionals who fly.

An old aviation adage says there is nothing more dangerous than a professional—doctor, lawyer, accountant—in a light plane.

The accident records provide countless examples of why the adage is true. Many professionals believe if they excel at one thing, they excel at everything. They rarely put as much effort into mastering flying as they did into mastering their profession, and so they fail to learn from their mistakes. This combination of professional, pilot, airplane, and overconfidence frequently ends badly, and many light planes are flown unceremoniously, often fatally, into the ground by well-educated, successful people.

So, let me tell you about one of the well-educated, successful people I had the most experience with—my dad, a doctor—who happened to be the exception to this rule.

Square-jawed, with salt-and-pepper hair and a deep voice, he seemed to be 10 feet tall. He had a prominent nose and large brown eyes that gave him an air of authority. While often serious, he loved a good joke, picking up many at the office or hospital, which he would gleefully share with anyone who would listen. He was an expert diagnostician with a curiosity a police detective would envy.

Unlike most professionals who become pilots, he was a pilot long before he was a physician. He joined the navy toward the end of World War II and flew torpedo bombers off the aircraft carrier U.S.S. *Randolph*.

Just flying on and off an aircraft carrier was pretty dangerous stuff. He used to say, "You never know fear like the fear of making a night carrier landing." The primary objective was to have your number of takeoffs equal your number of landings, and in that regard, he succeeded.

My dad used to say the thing he loved most about flying was that he could forget all about his earthbound problems and get a whole set of new ones. Despite his competence, he still occasionally got into difficult situations in airplanes, and he always learned from them. Once I became a pilot, I learned from my challenges, too.

Although he gave up flying after the military, he always wanted to return to the sky. Once established in his medical practice, with the family thriving, he found the time and an instructor, rented an airplane, and got his military pilot certificate reissued as a civilian license.

After a short time renting airplanes, my dad confidently decided he should buy one. He chose a small, used, single-engine, four-seat plane called a Mooney Super 21. The plane was cheap, fast, and tough to fly. That airplane type was known to attract a particular kind of pilot: frugal, daring, and up for a challenge. Thus, it was a match made in heaven—and that's where some of those pilots ended up.

It wasn't the Mooney's fault as much as it was the pilot's. Blaming only the Mooney would be as unfair as a carpenter who curses his saw for faulty construction when he should look no further than his own 10 thumbs. Still, several of my air-traffic controller friends tell me that in their unscientific survey, they've seen Mooney pilots do some of the dumbest things in the sky.

One reason I had no competition for a passenger seat in the Mooney was that at first, the rest of my family did not share my passion. They were scared to death of light airplanes. It took a lot of coaxing to get my two sisters, brother, or mother in that sporty little plane.

I was 12 years old when he got the Mooney, and I could barely see over the panel. My dad helpfully provided a pillow so I could peer out the windshield. He never let me take off or land, but I would dutifully steer the plane once we were airborne. I spent many Saturdays in the right seat of the Mooney, flying around with my dad out of the Philadelphia International Airport, trying to decipher the babble on the radio.

I recall two memorable trips in the Mooney where both my father and I learned a thing or two. One trip involved evacuating my sister from Dumbarton College in Washington, DC, in 1968. After the assassination of Dr. Martin Luther King Jr., riots broke out across the nation and especially in the Capitol.

I wanted to go.

"No passengers—this could be dangerous," my dad said, unaware that we universally considered any flight in the Mooney to be risky.

My father planned the trip like he was going to look for U-boats during the war, checking and rechecking the weather, route, and every contingency.

The next day he flew the little Mooney to Washington National Airport, which was easy to find because much of the city was in flames because of the riots, and the smoke was visible for miles.

It took forever for my sister to reach the airport. Streets were choked off with flaming wreckage, and the taxi driver struggled to find alternate routes, like an army ranger in a Humvee trying to escape Mogadishu. When she finally reached the airport, my father was waiting.

Kathryn greeted my father carrying her most coveted personal items: a suitcase the weight of a baby hippo full of albums by the Beatles, the Stones, Herman's Hermits, and other baby-boomer favorites.

With smoke looming over the horizon, my father hastily loaded the airplane. Actually, he *overloaded* it.

Maybe this was due to his wartime experience, but he didn't seem too concerned about overloading the airplane because, in the military, you had a parachute. The Mooney was most definitely parachute-free.

After a hasty preflight inspection, they boarded the Mooney. Because of the weight in the back, the nose was very high, and the strut on the nose landing gear was fully extended, barely in contact with the pavement.

"Daddy, I can't see over the nose," my sister said. "Why can't I see over the nose?"

"Not a problem," he said. "Once we get in and start the engine, it'll be fine."

It was anything but fine. They began the taxi with the tail inches from dragging on the tarmac, but that didn't seem to bother Dad. He was on a mission.

They were soon cleared for takeoff and were barely moving when the nose pitched up prematurely. Dad soldiered on, applying an enormous amount of nose-down pressure on the controls. They leaped into the air, almost dragging the tail in the process, but were airborne.

They made it home alive, and after the flight, which was characterized by unusual aircraft performance, my dad decided to check the weight and balance. He grabbed my sister's suitcase and weighed it.

"Huh, we were a little overweight," he said in his typical soft-pedaled, doctor's bedside manner. "Didn't know records weighed that much. Have to watch that next time."

On his next mission, I was allowed to come along. In an unusual move, my father somehow convinced my skeptical mother to join us on a family trip to West Palm Beach, Florida. She reluctantly agreed to fly in our relatively new toy. Everything went fine until our planned fuel stop in Charleston, South Carolina.

While on the ground there, we dutifully checked the weather. There was a cold front looming on the route to Florida. My mother was no meteorologist, but when she peered over my dad's shoulder at the weather map, she recognized the blue line with sharp triangles from watching the local weatherman on TV and told my father, "I'm taking Craig, and we'll fly the rest of the way on Delta. You can keep the bags with you." She kissed my dad and me, grabbed my bewildered younger brother, and waved goodbye over her shoulder.

I don't think she abandoned me because she liked my brother better; I just think she knew how important it was to me to spend every moment I could flying. I had no idea what I was getting into.

The first few minutes into the flight were fine. We were relaxed as we climbed to our cruising altitude. Then I saw ominous clouds ahead.

In a few minutes, we were enveloped. We banged along from one bulbous cumulous cloud to the next, the G-forces alternatively pulling and pushing us against our seat belts and the rain hissing hard against the windshield as we passed through the bigger clouds. Soon the sky turned charcoal, and the hiss turned to a roar as huge droplets hammered the tiny plane. There was an occasional flash of lightning that momentarily lit up the darkened cabin. We were close enough to nature's fireworks to sniff the chlorine-like smell of ozone from the lightning.

"I'm glad Mom isn't with us," Dad said in a strangely offhand manner given the circumstances.

Suddenly, the sky brightened once again as we popped out the front side of the cold front. My dad looked at me and smiled. "Wow, that was quite a ride, huh?"

We settled back in our seats and loosened our seat belts, and my dad poured himself a cup of coffee from his thermos.

The soothing purr of the engine was suddenly replaced by a whoosh as the propeller flattened and went from pulling us through the air to pushing hard into the air in front of us.

The engine had stopped cold.

My father had an aha moment and looked around the cockpit for a minute, trying not to spill his coffee. He then handed it to me, smiled, and, without a word, reached down to the floor to change fuel tanks. One had run dry.

The engine instantly sprang to life so quickly we didn't even lose much altitude.

"Now I'm *really* glad Mom isn't with us," he said as I handed the coffee back to him.

Thinking of my mom and Craig on that safe and luxurious Delta flight, I, too, had an aha moment. That said, I tightened my seat belt, crossed my fingers, and just smiled at my captain. Once again he was able to save the day and learn from the experience.

We all have strengths and weaknesses. But smart people know that striving for perfection is more important than achieving it. When you make a mistake, learn from it.

CHAPTER 4

AVOID THE HIGHWAY
TO THE DANGER ZONE

The problem with the world is that the intelligent people are filled with
doubts while the stupid ones are full of confidence.

—Anonymous

This story is about a couple of colorful characters who, despite
being successful at one thing, couldn't admit their shortcomings
at another—flying—with nearly fatal consequences. It's a great
reminder of how problematic and downright dangerous overcon-
fident people can be. They are everywhere. Don't let them
ground your dreams (or kill you!).

As adventurous as it was flying with my dad, two other
people made him look like Sky King—his good friend Bud Bartholomew and my uncle Bill. Both tremendously successful in
their day jobs, Bud and my uncle gave new meaning to the term
"fear of flying" because flying with them was often a hair-raising
experience.

Shortly after buying the Mooney, my dad realized this
little plane was quite expensive to own, so he brought in Bud as a
partner to help defray costs.

Bud was a bowling ball of a man. He was a short, bald, fiercely independent, arrogant, chain-smoking, scotch-drinking, wheeler-dealer small-business owner who ran a successful roofing supply company near Philadelphia called Safe-T. Bud wore poorly adjusted oversize black glasses that perpetually slid down his small nose, giving him an owlish appearance.

His house was a popular spot in the summer because he had a brand-new in-ground pool, the most spacious one in the neighborhood. He often bragged that although he had the biggest pool around, he didn't *pay* for the biggest pool.

On the day the contractors arrived to dig the hole, Bud wisely rolled out the red carpet. He had his wife prepared an elaborate breakfast for the workers, with eggs Benedict, omelets, and a wide assortment of pastries. Bud provided liberal rounds of Bloody Marys.

By the time they began to dig the hole, the excavator's spatial judgment and sense of responsibility were both impaired. He and his crew paid no attention to what was staked out and gouged a deep hole the size of a small open pit mine. A few days later when the concrete crew arrived, they had no choice but to fill the crater before them. The result was a pool big enough to accommodate Shamu.

While Bud congratulated himself for his crafty culinary sleight of hand with the contractor, I found it alarming. Purposefully impairing the men operating heavy equipment in your yard seemed like a questionable business decision. It was a harbinger of things to come.

Bud's small stature made him a natural fit for the Mooney, which was so tiny that flying in it with others was like riding around in a clown car with the LA Lakers. Nevertheless, to Bud, it was a spacious ride, and he was all about comfort.

I once asked him if he'd ever tried scuba diving. "Stephen"—as he called me with some formality—"I undertake only recreational activities that can be done from a chair." So flying was in, scuba was out.

Conversely, he drove an enormous Cadillac to symbolize his financial success. It was an El Dorado with jet-black paint and interior.

To his credit, Bud afforded me my first job, which, along with my lawn-cutting business, financed my flying lessons. I helped manufacture ladder hoists that roofers used to move supplies from ground level to the roof. It was an ingenious invention. Components included the ladder, cables, a cargo platform, and a 3.5 HP Briggs and Stratton lawnmower engine.

My job did not require a lot of skill. I would attach a vise clamp to the bottom of a ladder that contained a plate with two guide holes in it. I'd drill two holes, remove the vise clamp, and repeat until I burned out the drill. Then I would grab a new drill and continue the process until 5:00 p.m. I did this after school for many months, wearing out drill after drill, my eyes burning from the gasses that emanated from the overheated electric drill motors and breathing in thick, potentially toxic clouds of aluminum dust.

We often take on unpleasant, sometimes foul jobs on the way to achieving our goals. Whether it's earning money for school or training to get a certification or be mentored, not all jobs are glamorous. It's the price we pay for getting in the game. And that job helped finance my dream of becoming a pilot.

Bud wasn't a doctor-pilot, but he was a well-heeled professional with more money and arrogance than skill, a dangerous combination that led to problems.

On a sunny Saturday afternoon, Bud called my dad to inform him that he had landed the Mooney on its belly with the wheels up. However, it wasn't a case of just forgetting to put them down. Somehow, Bud managed to make himself the hero of the mishap.

The landing gear on the Mooney was controlled by a mechanical bar between the front seats called a Johnson Bar. Without getting too technical, the important thing was this: you had to make sure to snap the pin on the top of the handle into the receptacle at the base of the instrument panel to ensure the landing gear was down.

It was virtually impossible for such a simple mechanical system to fail. It had no hydraulic power, no electric servos, just an electric gear position light. It was purely mechanical. That said, you can't design a system to account for carelessness, incompetence, and arrogance.

To hear Bud explain it, he was coming in for a landing, conducting business as professionally as a B747 captain, judiciously running the before-landing checklist.

"Gas—on, mixture—rich, propeller—forward, flaps—set, gear—down and *locked.*"

Bud claims he thoroughly ran the before-landing checklist and saw a green gear down light, and just as the airplane touched down, the landing gear control bar pin somehow popped out of the receptacle, an unlikely scenario given the simplicity of the landing gear.

Heroically, and with surprisingly fast reflexes for someone so woefully out of shape, Bud continued to fly with his left hand on the control yoke while grabbing the landing gear bar with his right.

As the plane decelerated, lift dissipated, and weight won out. It became harder and harder to hang on to the bar, which grew heavier and heavier. Straining and breaking a sweat, Bud tried valiantly to hang on, but a lifetime of Pall Malls and Dewar's took a toll on his stamina. Soon the landing gear began to fold as the plane sank toward a belly landing, the prop tick-ticking against the asphalt runway as the bar finally slipped out of Bud's hand and slammed to the floor. The airplane skidded to a stop on its belly.

An observant air traffic controller, who must have witnessed the entire event, wisely called out the crash crew. Bud was quickly surrounded by fire trucks and men in silver fire suits at the Philadelphia International Airport.

There was no fire.

Bud calmly opened the airplane door, stepped onto the wing, and made the embarrassingly short second step from the wing to the tarmac, which was now on the same level. I think he would have lit up a Pall Mall just then, but the firemen obviously deterred him.

To my father's relief, the damage to the airplane was minor. There was no damage to the engine, and the few scraped panels and missing antennas could be replaced. There was also no damage to Bud's enormous ego.

When he recounted the harrowing event later, poolside, with a Pall Mall smoldering in one hand and a double Dewar's in the other, the story was quite a bit different from the report issued by the local Federal Aviation Administration (FAA) office.

Bud was a terrific businessman and a generous benefactor, but he didn't know his limitations. Although they make for great stories, people who don't listen, acknowledge, or learn from their failures will not help you find your bliss.

Another of my early pilot role models was my uncle Bill. He was also a doctor-pilot, but although he had all the confidence of a doctor, like Bud, he lacked my father's military flight training.

Uncle Bill, my mother's brother, was my favorite uncle. He was a tall, lean, affable family man living in Cherry Hill, New Jersey, with a successful medical practice. A master griller, we frequently enjoyed barbecues at his home on Saturday afternoons. He also had three kids, my cousins, all teenage boys like me.

The two best things about Uncle Bill were that he would take me flying when my dad couldn't, and he allowed my cousins to read *Playboy* magazine freely. That meant *I* could read *Playboy* freely, which made his house a very desirable spot for me.

Unfortunately, Uncle Bill could have been the poster child for the dangers of a professional man becoming a recreational pilot. He was a bit clumsy and usually had a small bandage on his head from bumping into something. He was in a hurry most of the time, running from the hospital to the office and invariably to the airport. Worst of all, he didn't have very much flying experience. At my young age, however, none of those things discouraged me from flying with him because I was on a mission to become a pilot.

Our families often spent the summers together on Lake Winnipesaukee in New Hampshire. One summer I rode with him from tiny Laconia Airport back to Philadelphia. Uncle Bill commanded the left seat, my father was in the right seat, and I sat in the back.

Since I was removed from the action, the comforting drone of the engine and the mild turbulence lulled me to sleep.

When I awoke an hour later, I noticed the sky getting very black as we approached our destination. There was some dramatic lightning arching from the clouds to the ground on all sides of us. Uncle Bill kept flying lower and lower to stay out of the churning black thunder clouds. We were following the Delaware River south, which he knew would eventually lead us to the

Philly airport. Soon we were so low I could easily spot the make and model of the cars below.

Flying low to avoid penetrating the clouds is known to pilots as "scud running." The idea is to get close to the ground without crashing into it or another airplane or obstacle. It is dangerous, usually illegal, and bat-shit crazy to do, but what did I know?

Suddenly, I looked out the front window and saw two red-and-white radio towers directly ahead of us. Not the tops of the towers—the middles of the towers. I vividly remember the red obstruction lights blinking cheerily. Before I could say anything, my dad barked, "Turn!" and Uncle Bill banked sharply to the left, narrowly missing them.

Those towers still exist just south of Camden, New Jersey, and loom to over 600 feet. What I didn't know is that there are also support cables that extend outward from those towers like tentacles, and we couldn't have missed them by much.

The rest of the flight was uneventful, and we soon landed in Philly. I felt a new appreciation for my dad's experience level compared to Uncle Bill's. Although he was a skillful physician, his real value was as an example of just how unpredictable and downright dangerous someone can be when they overestimate their skills.

It's a miracle both Uncle Bill and Bud survived their aviation pursuits, but it taught me a lifelong lesson about staying in your comfort zone and being aware of the strengths and weaknesses of those around you. I owe them both for that.

Despite bearing witness to these near-death experiences, my enthusiasm for flying was resolute. I had just turned 16, the minimum age for a student pilot's license, and I had logged plenty of time sitting in the right seat of our Mooney, learning what to do—and, more importantly, what not to do—in an airplane.

I amassed a small sum of money from working for Bud and from my three years in the lawn-mowing business. With a little cash and a lot of determination, I embarked on my quest to get my own pilot's license. I had learned plenty from my experiences with Dad, Bud, and Uncle Bill—cautionary tales that couldn't be found in a textbook. The next scary person I would fly with would be *me.*

CHAPTER 5

SEEK YOUR CIRCLE OF TRUST

Keep away from people who try to belittle your ambitions.
Small people always do that, but the really great make you feel
that you, too, can become great.

—Mark Twain

The world is full of people who will tell you that you can't achieve your goals. I know some people who listened to their detractors, and they failed to reach their potential. Choose wisely the people you listen to and your mentors even more carefully. Otherwise, you could be steered away from your dreams.

This brings us to my first flight instructor, Lester.

Les was a man whose mother named him well because the only way I could've learned "less" about flying from him was if I'd taught myself. On the bright side, he taught me a lot about sarcasm and the importance of finding positive influences.

I learned to fly at Chester County Airport in Coatesville, Pennsylvania. It was a good choice because the airport was small, close to my home, and had little air traffic. If you looked out on the horizon, you would see few things sticking up that you could fly into. That's always a plus.

I finally got together enough nerve and money to go for my first lesson. I walked into the dingy office at the flight school, and like most flight schools in those days, they had no idea of what a welcoming environment should look like. You almost felt that you were intruding, as if paying them money to teach you to fly was a privilege.

The furniture was worn, and the upholstery was sticky from years of spilled Coke, Sprite, and Mountain Dew. The ashtrays were full, and the room had the musty aroma of dried coffee and nicotine, with a subtle whiff of 100-octane aviation gasoline.

The lighting was terrible, and as I walked toward the counter, I heard something scuttle across the floor. I looked down, and a large rat tore around the corner of the counter and out the door into the hangar. An instant later, a 25-pound Maine coon cat followed in hot pursuit.

An older man was behind the counter, leaning against a filing cabinet with a smoldering Marlboro in one hand and a coffee cup in the other. Enough smoke surrounded him to qualify as a weather condition.

"Don't worry about that. We are in the country; you get rats. That's what the cat is for," he said in a low, smoker's croak. "So, what can I do for you?"

"I'd like to learn how to fly."

He paused, looked me up and down, and said, "How old are you?"

"Sixteen."

"What are you doing here in the middle of the day? Shouldn't you be in school?"

"I go to a special school."

"What do you mean, 'a special school'? Are you retarded?"

"No, special in that we have independent study. I don't always have to go to class during regular hours."

"Oh," he snuffed. He took one last drag off his cigarette, crushed it in the loaded ashtray, and said over his shoulder, "Hey, Les, come on out. We got a live one."

Les, my future instructor, came out from an office in the back.

He was tall and thin, about 27, with closely spaced, beady eyes that inspected me suspiciously from behind cheap plastic glasses.

"So you want to fly, huh? Are you even old enough to drive?"

"I've been driving for three months."

"Do you have money?"

"Yes, I have enough money to at least get started."

"Okay, if you can get here and pay for it, that's good enough for me," Les said. "Let's sign you up."

The smoking man was Paul, a charter pilot who flew the Learjet that sat in the hangar. In all the time I was at that flight school, I never actually saw him get into an airplane. He perpetually stood behind the counter, smoking a Marlboro and drinking coffee, apparently waiting to be called to fly a charter.

Les worked as a flight instructor solely to build flight time so he could move on to better jobs. Teaching required a lot of patience and a lot of talking, and the pay was at the bottom of the aviation food chain. As a charter pilot, all you had to do was fly. Naturally, he spent most of his time trying to score charters in the bigger twin-engine Piper Navajo, before graduating someday to the Learjet. Even at age 16, I could understand why I was playing second fiddle to Les's career aspirations.

My training aircraft was a Cessna 150. It weighed a mere 1,600 pounds and felt as durable as the lunar excursion module, which had skin about as thick as a sheet of Reynolds Wrap. Nobody wore headsets in those days, and once you cranked up the engine, the airplane was noisier than a freight train in a tunnel, so communication—an essential element of learning—was difficult.

The Cessna 150 is infamous for one thing in the history books. In 1994, an intoxicated Frank Eugene Corder intentionally crashed a Cessna 150 onto the South Lawn of the White House. Although he missed the building, he did manage to achieve one goal, which was to kill himself. No one else was injured, and damage to property was minimal. The incident, which took place on September 12, was eerily similar to the modus operandi of the September 11 terror attacks that would occur seven years later, almost to the day.

I would repeatedly test the structural integrity of that Cessna with my early landing attempts, which were more like assaults on the asphalt than the tender kiss of the runway I aspired to. As we rolled out after one not-so-gentle arrival, Les opened the window of the airplane, patted the side of the fuselage, and said, "I'm sorry. You'll be okay, old friend." The Cessna 150 turned out to be a durable trainer and ably tolerated my abuse.

One hot spring day, I was practicing maneuvers with Les. The afternoon thermals punched up at us from the cornfields below, and the controls danced in my hands. Nervous sweat formed on my forehead, and I cautiously reached up to open my air vent, which added more noise to the cockpit than fresh air.

We were practicing various maneuvers that were required for the flight check: slow flight, steep turns, ground reference maneuvers. All of them required a good deal of coordination between your hands on the controls and your feet on the rudder pedals. It all sounds easy until you throw in heat, turbulence, a screaming rattletrap of an airplane, and a screaming rattletrap of an instructor.

Suddenly, Les said, "Okay, I got it," and took the controls from me, as he often did to command my full attention.

"What sports do you play?"

That question struck me as a little off-topic. Then again, a lot of what Les said was off-topic.

"Uh, football," I said.

"What position?"

"Wide receiver."

"Well, I can't understand why someone coordinated enough to catch a goddamn football can't fly a Cessna 150."

A couple of weeks later, after the incredible sum of nine hours of flying time, Les declared that I'd never become a very good pilot because I was not coordinated enough. Of course, it never occurred to him that his instructional techniques—or lack thereof—could be part of the problem. Fortunately, I was blinded with singular determination, so I mostly ignored him.

Now, I didn't care about being the greatest pilot in the world. Charles Lindberg was a great pilot. Chuck Yeager was a great pilot. Neil Armstrong was a great pilot. I didn't want to fly solo across the ocean, fly faster than the speed of sound, or go to the moon. All I wanted was to be a skillful pilot, not famous for anything but getting safely and efficiently from point A to point B, and I wanted to have fun doing it.

Maybe I finally got the hang of landing, or maybe Les just couldn't stand to sit next to me any longer, but after one particularly good landing, Les said, "Pull over. I'm getting out. Take it around the pattern three times and then pick me up."

"Why three?"

"Well, if you do one or two, you might think it's just luck. If you do three, odds are you actually know what you are doing."

As happy as I was to be rid of Les, it instantly dawned on me there was nobody to bail me out if I screwed up.

Beads of nervous sweat formed on my upper lip as Les slammed the door, flipped me an okay sign with his hand, and strolled off the runway. He sat down in the turf next to the runway, pulled out a long piece of dry grass to chew on, leaned back, and smiled. I wasn't sure if he was rooting for my success or against it. Still, this was 100 percent on me now—no excuses and no help from Les.

I successfully made three takeoffs and landings by myself, amazed at how much less distracting it was without Les yelling in my right ear and how much faster the airplane climbed without his weight in the right seat.

I picked up Les, and as I taxied back to the flight school, he said, "Well, not the best landings I've ever seen, but at least you made it through alive."

When I showed up for my next lesson, Les was accompanied by another instructor, Mike. He was 18 years old but looked 14, skinny with a big smile and laid-back manner.

Les said, "Steve, meet Michael Johnson. I'm going charter full time, so Mike is now your instructor."

With that, Les shook my hand weakly and walked into the hangar. That was my last interaction with him.

Even though I had nothing to do with the change and was too young and stupid to request a new instructor, this was exactly what I needed. Les and I just didn't get along. He didn't want to be there, and it showed in almost everything he did.

"Good to meet you, Steve. Les said you just soloed, so I'm here to get you through to your license," Mike said.

I liked him immediately. We were both teenagers, loved airplanes, and suffered the skepticism every young pilot faced.

Mike had an easy disposition and clearly loved to fly. Lessons were actually enjoyable, and instead of hammering out one maneuver after another, we always took a few minutes during each flight to do some sightseeing and enjoy the experience.

My progress accelerated under his tutelage, and soon we were conducting flight planning and cross-country flights, a welcome change from practicing maneuvers. Finally, I was doing something airplanes were designed to do.

My first solo cross-country would be from Coatesville to Atlantic City, New Jersey. The school always selected this route because it was difficult to get lost. You took off, headed east until you hit the Atlantic Ocean, and the airport was either on the left or the right or directly below you.

After several months of training and a lot of encouragement from Mike, I passed my private pilot check ride and got my license. Had I listened to Les, I might have ended my flying career, and my life would have taken an entirely different turn. I am indebted to Mike for two reasons: helping me see I was more coordinated than I thought and giving me the confidence to realize Les was just plain wrong.

CHAPTER 6

SKYDIVE WITH A VAMPIRE

The best way out is always through.

—Robert Frost

I am a pilot, and I'm scared of heights.

I know, how could a pilot be afraid of heights? Truth is, a lot of us are. Put me in an airplane, and I'm fine. When I look out the window, it's almost like the earth is a picture, unreal. And I have the sturdy structure of the airframe all around me. However, put me on a cliff, bridge, balcony, steep hill, diving board, or stepladder, and I tense up. My legs get weak, and I imagine falling, which makes me more likely to do so. Something about the converging parallel lines I see from up high freaks me out.

Although ignoring fear was tempting, my passion for flying and the even *bigger* fear that it would stand between me and my dream compelled me to conquer it. I faced it head-on at 17 because after earning my pilot's license, my father thought I should learn aerobatics. He believed that perfecting rolls, loops, and spins would make me a more capable pilot. "You have to be comfortable upside down," he'd say, viewing all flight training through the lens of his initial pilot training in the US Navy.

The FAA has a rule that requires you wear a parachute while conducting such extreme maneuvers, just in case you screw up and rip the wings from the airplane. For that reason, despite my dread of heights, I decided I would try skydiving.

Since I was a minor, I needed parental permission. Unfortunately, my parents were not around. The summer before my senior year of high school, they announced they were sick and tired of the crime and crowding in the Philadelphia area and fled to the dry, wide-open spaces of Arizona. Since I had only one year of school left, I pleaded for them to let me stay. They agreed, as long as I lived with the parents of my good friend Eddie Robbins.

Unbeknown to my parents, I couldn't have asked for better temporary guardians during my senior year. Having already raised four kids, Eddie's folks, Murph and Jean, took a laissez-faire approach to parenting. They allowed events to take their natural course without interfering, so we pretty much did what we wanted. Asking them to forge the permission form, however, tested even their limits of leniency. I went to Plan B and enlisted my older sister, Kathryn, to forge the waiver.

I didn't know this at the time, but she had been schooled in the Palmer Method of penmanship by the very persistent nuns at her parochial school, which focused on moving the entire arm versus the fingers. All I knew was that she wrote just like my mother, who was also schooled by nuns. Later, I would learn that no one at the skydiving school gave a hoot what the signature looked like.

"You are sure you want to do this, Steve?" Kathryn asked.

"Yeah, sure. I hear it is pretty safe."

"Okay," she said as she forged Mom's signature, moving her entire arm in a circular pattern and not her fingers, in bona fide Palmer style. "If you kill yourself, Mom and Dad will have my ass."

From a practical standpoint, taking this skydiving course was a waste of time. If you flew badly enough to rip the wings from the airplane, you'd have a heck of a time trying to bail out. The aircraft would undoubtedly be spinning out of control as you watched your life, and the quickly rising ground, flash before your eyes.

Furthermore, in those days when you learned to skydive, your ripcord was physically attached to the airplane by a static cord, so as you departed from the safe cocoon of the cabin, your chute opened automatically. You don't learn a lot doing that. Remember all those war movies where paratroopers jumped bravely, one after another, out of a plane? Those were static jumps.

Even if you try skydiving now, you are not attached to the airplane on your first jump. You are attached to the instructor. While I'm sure that sounds comforting, it also teaches you little that's useful. Skydiving that way is like paying a Sherpa to drag your exhausted ass up to the top of Mt. Everest and then saying you climbed it.

Another emotional obstacle was the peer pressure from other pilots who looked at skydivers as crazy daredevils, jeopardizing their safety by being yet another thing in the sky you could collide with.

"Why jump out of a perfectly good airplane?" they'd say sarcastically.

Clearly, they thought skydivers were idiots.

Regardless of my doubts, I was sure I could enlist several of my high school friends to accompany me. The night before the adventure, I went to a little party with about a dozen of my friends. They all thought skydiving would be a blast, and I provided them with the necessary forms and details. Their enthusiasm, encouraged further by some bootlegged beer, was unrestrained.

"Yeah, I'm in. Sounds really cool," they each said.

The next morning it was a different story. Much of the enthusiasm of the previous evening had been fueled by the hops and a desire to impress several cute girls who were at the party. I called my friends, and one by one, they had some excuse.

"My parents won't let me."

"I have to mow the lawn."

"I have to babysit my brother."

"I have to write a paper for school."

My friend Javier Cabella was the most honest. "There is no way I'm doing that. You are crazy, but go for it. I hope you don't die."

Then he paused. "Hey. Why don't you ask my brother? He's a little crazy."

Javier came from a big Colombian family of nine kids, the biggest family in our high school. He loved to rattle off the names of his siblings as fast as an auctioneer: "Daniel, Carlos, Sebastian, David, Luis, Eliana, Angie, and Jean Paul." Jean Paul was one person, and I'm not sure why, after naming nine kids, Javier's parents decide to give number nine two.

To support such a large family, both parents worked long shifts as chemical engineers, and I rarely saw either of them.

They lived in an anachronistic Norman-style castle in sleepy suburban Upper Darby, Pennsylvania. The 40-room mansion, built in 1902, was the only home in the area big enough for that family.

Javier's brother David was born to live in that castle. He was tall, thin, and had straight brown hair in the style of the Beatles. His aquiline nose made him look a wee bit sinister. He made a lot of his own clothes, always black, including shirts with puffy sleeves and a cape he proudly wore to school. I would see him walking down Meredith Drive on his way home from school, cape billowing in the wind.

Until then, my most vivid image of David was when he gave an eerily authentic performance as Mordred in our high school drama production of *Camelot*. David was very good at portraying this mysterious character. When the play was over, he never seemed to come out of it.

The most remarkable thing about David, though, was that he slept in a coffin.

When I finally got up the nerve to ask him about it, David said, "It's not a coffin; it is a bed *shaped* like a coffin." Indeed, he had to have the coffin-shaped bed frame and mattress custom made.

However, I saw it once, and I'm telling you it looked like a goddamn coffin.

When you added it all up, any reasonable person would say David thought he was a vampire.

Still, I had to give him credit—David was the only guy who would go skydiving with me, and at this point, I couldn't be picky.

I called David, and without hesitation, he agreed to go. I believe he forged the parental consent form, and not in the Palmer method. We met up at the castle, and I drove us down the Schuylkill Expressway, across the Walt Whitman Bridge, and to a small airport in rural New Jersey.

The weather that day was perfect: clear skies, little wind, and a temperature of about 60 degrees. If we wanted an excuse to bail out of this endeavor, it wasn't going to be the weather.

We arrived at the school and checked in with the ancient receptionist, who was as wrinkled and desiccated as a dried apple doll. She examined our driver's licenses, and the next thing she wanted was the parental consent forms. We handed them over; she glanced at them and croaked, "That'll be $90. Each."

I didn't need to go through all the trouble of having my sister forge my mom's signature after all.

We retired to a small classroom with four other students, all young men in their twenties. There was not a woman in sight, which said a lot for the good judgment of that gender.

A few minutes later, our instructor, Roy, arrived, hobbling on crutches and wearing a cast on his leg that extended from his crotch to his ankle. He had the air of a drill sergeant, with a shaved head and square jaw to match.

"Now, I know what you are all thinking—that I did this skydiving. Rest assured, I didn't hurt myself jumping out of a plane," Roy said, convincing only David, who looked at me and smiled, his enthusiasm unwavering.

"So let's get started," Roy barked and clapped his hands together enthusiastically. I shot a worried look back at David.

Roy explained how the parachute worked. Once open, a small vent in the rear gave it modest forward velocity. When pulled, two handles above you turned you left or right, thereby giving you a modicum of control over where you landed. He also assured us that the person who packed the chutes, the rigger, was a true professional, but even if something did go wrong, you always had the reserve chute on your chest.

"What happens if the main chute gets tangled up? Won't the reserve chute get tangled up, too?" David asked.

Roy stopped in his tracks. "Oh, that can't happen," he lied.

Roy was quickly losing credibility with me, and with every word, my anxiety was rising. I began to sweat, not exertion sweat but nervous sweat, the kind that makes you reek like a high school locker room.

Roy then explained the process of exiting the airplane. We would sit on the floor of the high-winged Cessna 206—which had the right-side door removed—until it reached an altitude of 2,500 feet.

"Why 2,500 feet?" David interrupted.

"Well, it's high enough that you have plenty of time to get your chute open but not so high you might drift far from the landing zone," Roy said.

Once over the landing zone, our instructor would ensure that each of our ripcords was attached to the airplane, which meant we were also attached to the plane. We would then, one by one, scooch ourselves on our asses toward the gaping door and stick our feet out into the slipstream.

"Aren't you going to be our instructor?" David interrupted again.

Looking annoyed, Roy said, "No, I can't even get in the plane with this cast."

Getting back on topic, he continued, "Then you grab the wing strut, secure your feet on the metal step over the landing gear, and pull yourself out into the slipstream."

"Won't my face be really close to the propeller?" David asked.

Acrophobia plus fear of decapitation was making my palms slippery.

Roy sighed. "Yes, but as long as you are behind the wing strut, the propeller can't hit you."

Unconvinced, David rose and started to ask another question. Roy glared him back into his chair.

"What's your name?" Roy barked. I was beginning to think he was once a drill instructor.

"David."

"Okay, Dave..."

"It's David," he interrupted.

"Okay, *David*," Roy pronounced, addressing him directly just like a second-grade teacher. "Once you pull yourself out there, rotate your hands from a pulling position to a pushing position so you are ready to push off the strut. When your instructor slaps you on the leg, kick up your feet, then push on the strut as hard as you can," Roy explained, demonstrating with his hands. "It's very important that you kick your feet up first, and then push off. You don't want your chin to hit the metal step as you fall."

I reflexively touched my chin. I wasn't sure I understood the physics of all this.

"By the way, we will be in radio contact with you. You will have a small walkie-talkie receiver on your chest so we can radio instructions to you," Roy said.

"Can we talk back to you? Ask you questions?" David asked.

"No, you can't talk to us, but we can talk to you," Roy said, mustering what patience he had left. "That's when you go into the hard arch and spread position."

David laughed a little too loudly at the imagery. Everyone in the class stopped and glared at him.

Roy continued. "That means back arched, arms and legs spread. This position will cause you to fall chest first," he said, thrusting his chest out, chin up, arms flayed as his crutches clattered onto the floor and he teetered on his one good leg. "Like this."

David was trying it awkwardly from the seated position and inadvertently smacked me in the head.

"Sorry," he said.

Roy recovered his crutches and jammed them back under his armpits. "When the chute opens, locate the two handles above you called toggles. Grab the left one with your left hand and the right one with your right hand. Use these to steer toward the landing zone. Try to land into the wind," he said. "That's it!"

Roy stared directly at David. "Does anybody *else* have questions?

There were none.

We went outside with Roy, and due to his condition, another instructor showed how to land properly in a "parachute landing fall" so as not to end up like Roy. Each of us had the opportunity to jump off a small platform to practice the maneuver.

"This spreads out the impact on the largest possible area of your body, namely the medial gastrocnemius, tibialis anterior, rectus femoris, vastus medialis, biceps femoris, and semitendinosus muscles," Roy said, proud of his knowledge and exact pronunciation of the applicable body parts.

From there we ate a nervous lunch; put on jumpsuits, helmets, and goggles; and donned our parachute rigs. A feeling of dread grew from the pit of my stomach.

David and I were to go together on the first drop, accompanied by Melvin, our new instructor. Roy would watch from the ground.

We nervously crawled into the Cessna and strapped ourselves to the cool metal floor. I would be first out, so I was in front, Melvin was behind me, and David was in the back. Roy stuck his head in the door.

"You guys have fun now. Just remember your training."
Roy smiled at me. Then his smile faded as he glared at David. He
gave us a weak salute, turned, and hobbled away.

The pilot cranked the engine, which chugged to life with
a belch of acrid smoke that permeated the cabin and burned my
eyes, despite my goggles. Once we started moving, the smoke
cleared out, but I had never been in an airplane with the door off,
and even with a parachute on, it was unnerving. The propeller
looked dangerously close to us from inside the plane.

As we taxied out, I looked at David, huddled in the back.
He had a big grin on his face. I was not as sanguine. As a pilot, I
was always thinking about what could go wrong, and I could
think of about 32 things right off the top of my head. David,
however, was blissful in his enthusiasm for, and ignorance of,
what we were about to do. And like his brother Javier said, he
was a little crazy.

We took off and circled over the drop zone, the afternoon
thermals thumping at the little plane until we reached 2,500 feet.
It was loud, but Melvin yelled directly into my ear so I could hear.

"I'm attaching the static line," he said. "You okay?"

I gave a half-hearted shrug and a pleading look, much like
a doomed man about to be executed by guillotine, head already
locked in the lunette. In the back of my mind, I vowed never to do
this again.

Soon we were in position, and Melvin shouted the commands we'd learned about in ground school. I was in autopilot
mode now, trying not to let my imagination run away with me,
doing what I was taught.

"Seat belt off, slide your feet over the edge."

I complied quickly, remembering my training.

"Pull yourself out."

With a dry, sticky mouth, I steeled myself, grabbed the strut, secured my feet on the metal step, and heaved myself into the fierce slipstream. The air was much cooler at altitude than it felt on the ground. Not looking down, I rotated my hands on the cold metal from the pulling position to the pushing position. There was no way to get back into the airplane now as my feet teetered on the precarious step. There was only one way out, and that was down.

Melvin slapped my leg and yelled, "Jump!"

I gritted my teeth, kicked up my back feet, and pushed off the strut with all my might, my chin clearing the step by about a foot.

Suddenly, at that instant, this whole thing seemed like a terrible mistake. As my friends who are pilots would say, I had just jumped out of a perfectly good airplane! Had I not relieved myself that morning, I would have emptied my bowels into my jumpsuit.

I spastically assumed the poorest and most asymmetrical hard arch and spread ever. Instead of falling chest-first, I started rolling slowly to my right. The free-fall portion was only a few seconds, but it felt longer than High Mass on Easter Sunday.

Thankfully, the static line jerked the ripcord from my chute, and miraculously it opened. Since I was half on my side, it jerked me not only up but also to the side. From the ground, I'm sure I looked like a crazed marionette as I jiggled below the opening parachute.

Looking up, I saw my fully inflated orange parachute. I quickly located the toggles and got my bearings, now secure in the knowledge I was going to live after all.

For the first time, I took a good look at the ground, and it appeared a lot more terrifying than when viewed from the safe confines an airplane. When hanging below the parachute, I had no sensation of descending. I felt like I was trapped, suspended in midair.

Despite that, per Roy's instructions, I toggled to the right a bit and steered toward the drop zone, which was marked with a big white X on the field below me. Unfortunately, it looked like a long way off.

Quite literally out of the blue, I heard Roy's scratchy voice emanating from the radio on my chest. He sounded as clear and understandable as a weak Mexican AM radio station. Although I couldn't understand a word, the tone of his garbled chatter sounded encouraging. Had I been able to respond, I would have had a few choice words for Roy, which is probably why the radio wasn't two-way.

Closer to the ground, I started to feel that I was descending and began to make out where I would land. It appeared I was headed for the intersection of a two-lane road and a barbed-wire fence. The pilot had dropped us too far south. At this point there was little I could do, but I knew that no matter what, I'd rather be hit by a car than have my gonads impaled on rusty spikes.

Luckily, I cleared both, barely making it to the corner of the field. Touching down, I executed a clumsy but survivable parachute landing fall.

As I gathered up the parachute, a voice called to me.

"Steve, hey, up here. Isn't this incredible!" It wasn't the radio; it was David descending quickly, right for me. "The feeling of free-falling was amazing...."

I ducked just in time, and his foot passed inches from my helmet. His voice rose and fell in pitch as he flew by, just like a passing train. He flopped down and rolled into a ball, probably because he was still talking instead of paying attention to his parachute landing fall, getting tangled up in the rigging.

I removed my parachute and jogged a few short steps to flip David from his stomach onto his back, unwinding the parachute cords that enveloped him. With wide-open eyes and a lopsided grin, he said, "It was like flying!" I'll bet he was thinking about bats, but I didn't say anything.

"We were high above everyone and everything!" he gushed.

We gathered our things and walked toward the van that came to recover us.

"David, thanks for coming with me," I said.

He stopped and placed his hand on my forearm. "Do you want to go again?" he asked hopefully.

"No. That's okay, David. Like my pilot friends say, 'Why practice something you did right the first time?'"

While my vampire friend would have been content to relive the adrenaline rush of the jump over and over, I knew I would never do it again. Did it make me a better pilot? Probably not, but the experience helped me face my fear and gain the confidence I could do anything if I put my mind to it. Don't let your fears be the limiting factor that pushes your dreams just beyond your grasp.

CHAPTER 7

GET SCARED SMART

By seeking and blundering we learn.

—Johann Wolfgang von Goethe

After I earned my pilot's license, I couldn't wait to take someone flying with me. Unfortunately, at 17 years old, with about 60 hours of flying experience, my entire pool of potential passengers was limited to foolhardy teenagers with irresponsible parents. One such teenager was Eddie Robbins.

Before I took Eddie for a ride, I wanted to complete my father's qualification to-do list by learning aerobatics: loops, rolls, and split Ss.

I spent about 10 hours in an aerobatic Cessna 150 with another instructor, Bill, at Chester County Airport. Bill seemed to be pretty good at it, although I don't know his qualifications. He wasn't in the military and didn't go to flight test school. For that reason, I think he may have been self-taught. Anyway, after a while, he deemed me fit to practice by myself, which was a bit premature.

The first person I would demonstrate my newfound talents to was Eddie.

I'd known Eddie for most of my life. We grew up together in Wallingford, Pennsylvania, and went to the same school, although he was a year behind me. Most importantly, his family's generosity was the sole reason I was able to remain in Pennsylvania after my father, now a bolo-tie-wearing closet cowboy, decided to uproot the homestead and move to Arizona.

Like Bud Bartholomew, Eddie's father, Murph, was a successful small-business owner and a self-made man. He grew Robbins Motor Transportation from one truck up to about 150 and spent nearly every waking hour attending to work. He had a telephone to his head almost all the time and was usually yelling at someone who owed him money.

Gruff and informally educated, Murph believed more in hard work and sacrifice than in academics. He was also extremely generous. Despite our total lack of experience or aptitude, he would provide well-paying summer employment to just about any of us who applied.

The entry-level job was to pick up nails in the staging yard to head off flat tires before they occurred. As easy as that job was, one of his clever grandkids later figured out how to make it even easier. He fitted the bottom of a forklift with a giant magnet and drove it across the lot, reducing a three-hour job to about 15 minutes of very light work.

Murph had no patience for people who complained. For example, if a worker complained about the condition of one of the forklifts, he'd say, "I don't want to hear it. When I used to load trucks, *these* were my forklifts," extending his two muscular arms.

Speaking of machines, Eddie had a reckless fondness for them, especially ones that moved. When he was younger, his father bought him a mini motorcycle, which he rode ferociously around the elementary school parking lot. He was considerate enough to engage in this dangerous activity in the late afternoon, long after the younger kids were gone.

As he grew older, Eddie amassed a collection of automobiles, ranging from Porches to BMWs, all of which he drove fast. Shortly after acquiring a center-engine Porsche 944, he spun out on a damp road, somehow blowing out the very expensive back window.

While interested in airplanes as machines, he never got around to learning how to fly. He did so vicariously through me, which, given the Porsche incident, was probably a boon to all those people he never flew over.

The Robbins home had a fully furnished walkout basement decorated like an authentic old West saloon, complete with a bar, card tables, an upright piano, and light fixtures made of wagon wheels. Murph and Jean kept the basement bar well stocked with beer and liquor, with no apparent method of accounting for it, which resulted in an incredible level of what retailers call "shrinkage." Of course, that's precisely what made it a natural gathering place for the neighborhood teenagers.

I remember sitting in my room one night, studying for an exam, when Eddie walked in, sat down, and cracked open a Schlitz beer that he had stolen from the basement cooler.

"Eddie, I gotta study," I pleaded with him.

"No, you don't. You're a senior; it doesn't matter anymore." He slurped the icy brew, setting another one down on my desk.

"I can't. No way. Maybe later," I said.

"Have it your way, then." He walked out, leaving the beer dripping condensation temptingly on the desk.

I think my ability to resist that Schlitz elevated me in Eddie's eyes, even though he had to drink alone that night. Maybe it's one reason he had so much confidence in me.

Eddie's attitude was risky, though, because the typical teenage boy's brain is thus occupied: 60 percent sex, 20 percent eating, 10 percent getting out of high school, and 5 percent zits. That left only 5 percent for flying. Despite these facts, Eddie was all in.

We drove from Media to Coatesville, Pennsylvania, in my parents' gas-guzzling Buick Electra 225, which they had left behind as a consolation prize when they abandoned me for Arizona. This was no easy feat because it was 1973, and we were amid the Arab Oil Embargo. There were lines around the block to get gas, and I had to wait one hour just to fill up. I almost killed the guy in front of me as he pumped only about four gallons of fuel into his car. This was why we had lines! People were filling up much more frequently than they needed to ensure they would not run out of gas, which created more demand at the pump, which created long lines, and so on. It was easier to get gas for the plane than to fuel an automobile.

Along the way, I gave Eddie an idea of what we would do. When we arrived, I got the keys to our plane, grabbed two parachutes, and walked out to the waiting aircraft. I handed Eddie his parachute.

"What's this for?"

"Oh, it's just a regulatory requirement; don't worry. It's sort of a last resort kind of thing," I said, "in case the wings come off or something."

I opened the door to begin the preflight inspection. I could see Eddie eyeing the two red escape handles.

"Why are these red handles connected to the door hinges?" Eddie asked.

"Oh, you use them if you have to make a quick exit from the airplane. Just pull on the handle, and the door falls off," I said as if I was describing how to use a bottle opener.

"Why would you want to jump out of the airplane?"

Again, being vague, I mumbled, "In case the wings come off or something."

I could see a little chink in Eddie's resolve, but he'd come too far to leave now.

We hopped in, cranked up the engine, and were on our way. We climbed up to 3,000 feet to start the fun.

We began with a few aileron rolls. You nose down to gain speed, pitch up about 30 degrees, and turn the wheel full right while you watch the horizon twirl before your eyes, ending up level again. That's pretty easy as long as you don't let the nose drop.

I remember my instructor bailing out of a few of these maneuvers halfway through, while inverted. He'd simply flip upside down, and instead of continuing the roll back to level, he'd stop rolling and pull back on the yoke, turning the roll into a half loop. That's called a split S, half roll and then half loop.

What he failed to tell me, and I failed to notice, was that you need to be going very slow when you decide to do the half loop. Why? Because the airspeed builds up at a startling rate as the airplane passes the vertical. You want to minimize the amount of time you are pointed directly at the ground. That 5 percent of teenage brain allocation was just not enough.

Two things can cause the wings to come off when doing aerobatics. One is exceeding the maximum allowable airspeed, and the other is exceeding the maximum allowable G load on the airframe. On the next maneuver, I would test both of those limits.

"How about another aileron roll, Eddie?" I asked.

"Sure, it's pretty fun."

"Okay, look for other traffic. All clear? Here we go." I began.

I put the nose down to build speed, pitched up 30 degrees, and rolled. As I rolled, and the airplane inverted, I inadvertently let the nose fall a bit. So, emulating my instructor, I stopped rolling and started pulling back for the split S. Unfortunately, I was going way too fast.

In slow motion, I remember the airspeed needle winding clockwise toward the maximum speed limit at an incredible rate. The only thing I could do to slow it down was to pull through the vertical as quickly as possible. Except that meant putting more G loads on the airplane. With the speed heading for supersonic, I had no choice. I pulled as hard as I dared, balancing speed and G-forces, and tried not to exceed either limit. The G-forces pressed us hard into our seats, and we both groaned from the stress as I pulled out of the dive.

Luckily, the speed stayed below the maximum, but we pulled four Gs in the process, close to the maximum allowable for the tiny Cessna.

As my heart rate slowed to under 200, I glanced over at Eddie.

He didn't look good.

A quick biology tutorial: when you're nauseous, blood moves out of your head into your stomach, where it is needed. Eddie's normal face color was pink, but he went from pink to a yellowish tint as the blood drained south. The veins in his face were blue, and the blue-tinged veins under the now-yellow skin made him look green. Eddie was literally green with airsickness.

Tactfully ignoring my near attempt to kill us both, Eddie just said, "I think we should probably land now."

To Eddie's credit, he accompanied me on more docile cross-country flights where we kept the wings level with the horizon. After what I'd put Eddie through, that's a true friend.

We flew up the coast to New Haven, Connecticut, to visit his sister. Another favorite trip was to Hershey, Pennsylvania, where we toured the chocolate factory and laughed at the streetlights shaped like Hershey kisses, the aroma of cocoa in the air. Or we'd just drill holes in the sky and sightsee like I used to do every lesson with my flight instructor Michael.

As proficient as I had become with basic flying, I knew I needed to pursue more advanced licenses. I'd been accepted to several colleges and chose the University of Arizona so that I could pursue flying in its characteristically good weather. And my major screw up with Eddie taught me more than another 10 hours of flying with Bill.

My takeaway? Learn the rules, practice your lessons, pay attention to the details, but also be wise enough to respond to a challenge when things don't go as planned. That will happen more than you think.

I knew the next phase of my training would be difficult, but I had no idea how high the bar would be set by my next instructor.

CHAPTER 8

GOOD ENOUGH WON'T DO

If you chase perfection, you often catch excellence.

—William Fowble

Like Aristotle, Voltaire, and Sting, some exceptional people are known only by their monoym. Lum was one, and he had a profound impact on me.

Someone once told me I should choose my heroes carefully. That didn't mean much to me until later in life when I realized just how few people really deserve to be admired and emulated. Without question, Lum was well qualified.

An imposing figure, G. A. Lum Edwards ran Arizona Frontier Aviation in Tucson, Arizona. It's where I continued my flight training and landed my first paying pilot job as a flight instructor. He was well over six feet tall, laconic, spoke with a gravelly voice, wore a tie no matter how hot it was, and insisted that anyone working for him do the same. He would often gaze down on you silently through black-framed glasses with the kind of stoic glare you expect from movie heroes. Among other honors, he was inducted into the Arizona Aviation Hall of Fame in 2008.

Lum was also an FAA examiner, which made him godlike in the eyes of aspiring pilots. The FAA gave him the authority to

administer the tests that granted you various levels of pilot certification. In a way, being tested by Lum was like going to the dentist. The procedure was painful, but you were better off for the
experience in the long term.

His deadly serious comportment vis-à-vis flying was
probably a result of his start in aviation.

Like my dad, Lum learned to fly during World War II. He
participated in one of the most dangerous missions in the war
flying cargo across the eastern end of the massive Himala-
yan Mountains, which pilots nicknamed, with typical ironic un-
derstatement, "the Hump."

After the Japanese blocked the Burma Road, the air route
from India to China was the only way to supply the Chinese war
effort of Chiang Kai-shek and the US Air Force against the Japanese. Almost everything needed to support a war was shipped in
this manner, including practical equipment like guns, ammuni-
tion, mortars, and hand grenades. Other necessities, like food,
fuel, newspapers, toilet paper, beer, at least one piano, and over
3,000 army mules tended by Chinese "cowboys," also made the
trip.

Flying over the Himalayas in the propeller airplanes of
the day was downright suicidal. The Himalayas are home to some
of the highest mountains on the planet, with over a hundred
peaks raggedly jutting above 23,000 feet. Most of the airplanes in
use back then couldn't claw their way to 23,000 feet, forcing pilots to fly through the lower, dangerous, narrow mountain passes.

Challenges included inaccurate charts, lack of weather
information, and very few navigation beacons. Those that were
positioned to guide pilots safely through the mountain passes
might be moved by crafty Japanese soldiers to point airplanes
fatally into the side of a mountain.

Pilots had to deal with severe turbulence, with some aviators reporting being flipped upside down by wind gusts. Hail and sleet pummeled the planes, torrential rains lashed at them, and ice built up on the wings. Pilots nicknamed the perilous peaks "cumulo-granite." And there was always an occasional Japanese fighter plane that shot down unarmed cargo aircraft, which were no match for the small attackers.

It was a dangerous place to fly. Some airplanes went down in the mountains or in the thick jungles that lay below, called the "aluminum trail." With spare parts in short supply, teams were often sent into the foothills to recover what they could. The accidents spawned a craft industry among the mountain villagers, who produced aluminum artifacts from crash site debris.

Due to the heavy casualties, green replacement pilots fresh from military flight school were sent to fly early missions. I'm guessing this is where Lum learned how to deal with inexperienced pilots. It is no surprise he would dedicate his life to teaching pilots how not to crash and fail anyone on a check ride who showed signs that they might.

Lum spent part of his time instructing, part of his time administering check rides, and the rest of the time figuring out how to make money with the flight school. AFA, as we called it, was run like a tight ship. No dirty ashtrays, stained furniture, or rats lurked in the waiting room. Lum kept the place looking sharp, unlike my first flight school back in Pennsylvania. As a business, however, it was tough to make a decent return.

I was fortunate to have Lum as one of my instructors because he didn't take on many new students. His discipline and professionalism had a very positive influence on me, even though my ego often suffered from his withering debriefings after a lesson. That's the tricky thing about learning from mentors. To benefit from their wisdom, you often must take your lumps and accept constructive criticism. You won't break, and it always makes you stronger in the bargain.

More than once I would become overwhelmed by the maneuver or task. As soon as I had things under control, like making a nice 60 degree banked steep turn, right on altitude and right on airspeed, Lum would slap a piece of paper over a crucial instrument, and things would go to hell.

He never left you alone, always adding another layer of complexity to tax you to just short of exasperation. I often felt like a man with his head barely above water, and just as I got in a few gasping breaths, Lum would toss me a 12-ounce bag of buckshot. It wouldn't sink you, but it sure made you kick harder.

No matter how difficult things got, it would never be as bad as flying the Hump. Lum would remind you of that every time you reached task saturation. At the slightest protest, he would fire off his favorite question.

"Is anyone shooting at you?" he'd ask.

I'd always reply, "No."

He'd say, "Then it can't be that bad."

Lum was also pragmatic, cautious, and thorough, with a good deal of skepticism. Those qualities probably helped keep him alive through over 30,000 hours of flying. Here's a good example.

Cessna once came up with a great airplane design that promised to improve safety in twin-engine light planes. Instead of placing one engine on each wing, which created a tendency to yaw when one failed, it designed the Skymaster, which had one engine on the front that pulled and one on the back that pushed. In this configuration, if an engine failed, there would be none of the yawing and subsequent control problems of a conventional twin.

This unusual engine configuration generated many slang nicknames for the aircraft: Push-Pull Cessna, Mixmaster, and Suck-Blow among them.

If you lost an engine in the Skymaster, even though the design solved the control problem, it didn't fix the performance problem. When one engine quit, you still cut your number of power plants in half. And most of those light twins had minimal performance on one engine.

Like all innovations, there are always drawbacks. There was no back window, so you couldn't see the rear engine. More than one pilot forgot to start that engine—out of sight, out of mind—and tried to take off with only the visible forward engine operating. The wise folks at Cessna strongly recommended that pilots start the rear engine first to avoid such embarrassment.

To sell Lum on the stability and performance of the Skymaster, the Cessna demo pilot took him for a ride in the new plane. But instead of taking off conventionally, with both engines operating, he had another idea.

"We will start both engines, but I'm going to use only the front engine for takeoff," he told Lum. "I'll leave the back engine at idle."

Lum was skeptical but decided to give it a try. After all, he had a duplicate set of flight controls in front of him and could take command if things went badly.

They taxied out and were cleared for takeoff on Tucson's two-mile-long runway. The demo pilot applied full power on the front engine and left the aft engine at idle.

They rolled and rolled, with minimal acceleration. The runway distance-to-go markers flashed by: 10,000, 9,000, 8,000 feet remaining. They were barely going 50 knots, well below flying speed. 6,000, 5,000, 4,000, and they were up to 60 knots—

still too slow. With the marker for 3,000 feet flying by and the end of the runway clearly in view, Lum had seen all he needed.

"That's just about enough for me!" he said as he pulled the front throttle to idle, aborting the takeoff demonstration.

That's how Lum kept alive all those years, always on his toes and ready to pull the plug. I took note of that and tried to emulate him. I don't think I could have chosen a better role model.

If you don't already have a role model or mentor, I encourage you to find one. Increase your benefit by locating ones who have different strengths so you can expand your capabilities. There is no such thing as too much excellence.

CHAPTER 9

WHEN THE STUDENT BECOMES
THE MASTER

To teach is to learn twice.

—Joseph Joubert

The following sentence will make no sense whatsoever. *The easiest job to get in flying requires the least amount of experience and pays the least amount of money—teaching other people how to fly.*

With just a few hundred hours of flying time and a new instructor license, you can make a paltry living passing along your newfound knowledge to others. While they learn, you learn; their mistakes become your realizations, and your skill improves seemingly without lifting a finger.

Despite Lum's nitpicking assessment of my flying skills, he must have thought I was okay, because once I earned my instructor license, he immediately hired me. As I said, it's an easy job to get.

With every bit of respect to those intrepid souls who teach for a living, imparting knowledge to people who have little is a grind. While teaching may cause you to rethink your life choices several dozen times, it's an excellent way to reinforce the basics as you strive for perfection.

The best way to know you understand something is to be able to explain it to others. I never regretted my time instructing, although I spent most of my time talking, not flying. The only time an instructor gets to fly is when demonstrating a maneuver, and those opportunities are rare. I didn't plan a career sitting in a cockpit watching other people fly. I wanted to be the guy doing the actual flying.

New instructors got the novice pilots who were working toward their basic certificate, the Private Pilot License. You usually fly the smallest and most uncomfortable airplane, my old friend the Cessna 150. Teaching basic flying was as exhausting as ditch digging in the Arizona caliche and as stressful as being a firefighter during an arson outbreak.

First, it was hot and bumpy, and there was no air-conditioning. If the temperature on the ground was 110°F, which it often was, you didn't get much relief as you climbed to a higher and cooler altitude. The air cools down about 3.5°F for every thousand feet, so the coolest it gets is still north of 90. Moreover, if you flew any time after about 10:00 a.m., the broiling desert sun heated the ground, which sent up uneven columns of hot air that beat you around more relentlessly than a prizefighter. I'd look enviously at the Continental and American jets that shared the airport, longing for the air-conditioned comfort of those cockpits.

Students were continually thinking up new ways to kill you. They didn't do it on purpose; they just made mistakes. You had to pay close attention at every moment. The trick was to let things deteriorate near the point of disaster without intervening. If you took over too soon, the student wouldn't learn anything. If you let it go too far, you might have a lot of explaining to do to the FAA and the student's next of kin, assuming you were in any condition to talk.

A good example of this quandary occurs when teaching the landing. The idea behind landing a small plane is to glide it nose down to the runway. At the exact right moment, raise the nose, remove the power, and allow the main wheels to kiss the runway surface—gently. If you start raising the nose too soon, you will run out of airspeed and drop the airplane onto the runway—hard. If you start raising the nose too late, you will prang nose-wheel-first onto the runway, usually resulting in a big bounce back into the sky and subsequent double bounce of the nose gear on your second iteration, which will continue until you either get it under control or break off the nose gear.

Nevertheless, the most maddening thing to deal with when teaching new pilots is the concept of "right rudder."

When flying a propeller-driven airplane, you need to use your feet on the rudder pedals to counteract the propeller motion in a climb by applying right rudder. If you don't, the airplane climbs in an uncomfortable and uncoordinated lean to the right. It is the thing that new pilots forget to do repeatedly. I used to call it "pilot polio," because they were flying as if they were dead from the waist down.

As a result, the two most common words uttered by flight instructors in primary flight training are right rudder. I cannot tell you how many times I recited that mantra of basic flying. My college roommates told me that I even said it in my sleep, loudly enough to wake them. If you ever want to impersonate a flight instructor, and have no flying experience whatsoever, just climb in the airplane with the student and keep saying, "Right rudder!" You will have instant credibility.

Despite these challenges, I was grateful for the flying time and manically scheduled myself to be available whenever I was not in my college classes. In the summer, with no college, I would book two-hour blocks starting at 6:00 a.m., with my last student ending at 6:00 p.m. and no lunch break. It is during this period that I gained an appreciation for how pissed-off dentists get if you are a no-show. I was paid only if I flew, so when a student stood me up, it was usually impossible to plug another student into my schedule. No student, no pay was not an economically viable option.

Thank God for one of my students, Jerry Toci. Jerry was a ticket agent for Hughes Air West who regretted never making it as an airline pilot. By then he was too old, so he used his job at the airline to fund his flying hobby. He gave me a great piece of advice: do one thing every day to get you closer to your goal.

The other thing Jerry did was feed me. He would come by AFA with uneaten crew meals and snacks he swiped from Hughes Air West airplanes. He knew I was poor and hungry, and sometimes that was the only thing I ate during the day. I am amazed I never got sick from eating all that leftover food. Jerry also misappropriated half-consumed bottles of wine, which I enjoyed with my friends in the evenings.

Blessed relief from the drudgery of instruction came when you finally got the chance to fly a plane. A friend's father owned a nice new single-engine, six-seat airplane called a Cherokee Six. He graciously allowed us to fly it if we paid for the fuel.

One summer afternoon we flew the plane—and our girlfriends—from Tucson to Lake Havasu City, now the home of the London Bridge. We felt like a couple of high rollers, pretending to be the spoiled rich kid owners of the plane, flying in for a weekend of frolic on the lake.

Those forays were few and far between, though, and I spent most of my time making takeoffs and landings at Tucson International Airport, flying to the nearby south practice area, where we repeated maneuvers ad nauseam, and teaching pilots how to navigate from one airport to the other. These trips were and still are called, inaccurately, cross-countries. Rather than spanning the continent, they covered only a few hundred miles.

We called the south practice area the SPA for two reasons. First, that was its proper abbreviation, and second, the afternoon desert heat made it feel like you were in one. It was a section of desert over which I spent innumerable hours. The area was designated as such because the few residents below could best tolerate noise or an airplane falling out of the sky.

Many days I would stare out the side window, straight down, to relieve my boredom while some student demonstrated slow flight for the hundredth time. The desert floor would rotate below me with every turn right and left. Below there were ranches, strip mines, washes, saguaro cacti, plenty of paloverde trees, and the occasional nuclear missile silo, with an innocuous chain-link fence surrounding a benign-looking concrete pad. It belied the size of the extensive compound beneath it that supported one leg of the nuclear triad. Even though I was pretty sure they would not be launching any missiles, superstition and my recollection of the Cuban Missile Crisis kept me from flying directly over them.

The most prominent feature of the desert was what is now called the Asarco open pit copper mine. These massive holes in the ground were punctuated by tailing ponds the color of the Caribbean—green, blue, and teal—and somehow their color refreshed me in the blazing heat of the little cockpit.

I enjoyed some welcomed relief when most of my students got to the phase in their training where they needed to stay next to the airport and practice nothing but takeoffs and landings. One day my mind was numb as I realized that by noon I had already endured about 30 takeoffs and landings. More out of boredom than anything else, I decided I needed to set a personal record for the highest number of takeoffs and landings in a day. There would be no SPA for me, no cross-countries, just takeoffs and landings.

Later that afternoon one of my students objected to my plan.

"I want to practice maneuvers today," he whined.

I said, "How many times do you think you will do steep turns after you get your license?"

He shrugged.

I said, "Right. How many times will you do takeoffs and landings?"

"Every time?" he said.

"Right. We are doing takeoffs and landings today."

In retrospect, I realize that wasn't very professional of me, but heck, you just can't have enough takeoff and landing practice. I'm very proud of the fact that I rode along for 72 of them, a personal record I have never come close to matching in any airplane.

I hope the students I taught learned something of value from me. I know I learned a lot from them. And sometimes you learn some painful lessons by watching pilots in other airplanes.

One hot June day, I got the mother of all lessons from an unlikely source: an experienced airline pilot.

The typical afternoon monsoon thunderstorms were popping up around the airport. Often, they are more dust than monsoon because it is so arid in Arizona that the rain sometimes evaporates before it ever hits the ground. These are known paradoxically as "dry" thunderstorms.

As I peered out the AFA office window, I noticed the wind picking up, and the dust started to blow with great gusto.

In fact, it got so windy and dusty that no pilot would attempt a takeoff—except one.

A Continental Airlines B727 taxied out, not to the standard long northwesterly runway but to the much shorter southeasterly runway, which the gusty and unpredictable wind was favoring.

Soon the wind was over 30 knots, with gusts considerably higher. There was a Cessna 172 parked outside right in front of me. Fortunately, it was securely anchored to the pavement, but due to the ample wind and slack in the chains, it briefly lifted off the ground.

Meanwhile, the B727 pilot elected to commence his takeoff as he should, into the wind. I watched it roll and roll, then disappear as it passed the hump in the middle of the runway.

Lum joined me at the window.

"This don't look good," Lum said in his typical laconic, understated way.

Many anxious seconds went by as we waited for the big jet to reappear.

Finally, it emerged with a bright flash enveloped in a cloud of dust, and it was very, very low—so low it had struck two 39-foot-high electrical poles, 71 feet from the end of the runway. The flash was caused by the electrical arc when the cables were severed.

The plane slowly and inexorably rose from the desert floor trailing fuel, which was pouring out of a hole in the left wing. By now the wind had subsided, and the plane made a wide left turn and landed on the long northwesterly runway. Thankfully, no one was hurt.

With the real-time drama over, Lum and I jumped in my car and drove to the end of the runway. There was already a crowd gathering, and soon the sheriff's deputies arrived. The 39-

foot-tall telephone poles were splintered and now stood only about five feet tall.

The live electrical wires were strewn about, and the sheriff did his best to keep people away from them. There were also aluminum pieces scattered about, and one enterprising soul was loading the valuable scrap aluminum into the back of his pickup truck. I got the sheriff's attention and said, "I think the National Transportation Safety Board might need that stuff."

It turned out the scrap metal was the left landing gear door, which the sheriff reclaimed from the industrious scavenger. The collision had also damaged the fuselage, flaps, landing gear, and leading and trailing edges of the wings.

The crew had encountered severe wind shear, a rapid shift in wind direction or velocity. The strong headwind at the beginning of the takeoff had shifted to a tailwind as the aircraft rolled down the runway, acutely degrading its performance. The pilot was unfamiliar with the airport, and he turned onto the runway, not noticing the additional 500 feet of runway to his right. He had used only 6,500 feet of the 7,000 feet of runway available.

My big takeaway was this: when nobody else is taking off, maybe you shouldn't, either.

I continued to work as an instructor, and some of my colleagues knew of my dream of becoming an airline pilot. One older, bitter instructor was not exactly encouraging. "The airlines only hire ex-military pilots," he told me when learning of my aspirations.

With that vote of no confidence, I soldiered on.

Eventually, I started teaching pilots for more advanced ratings in the bigger planes. However, like Les, what I really had my eye on was the sweet new Cessna 402 that the flight school had acquired to conduct Forest Service charters. It was the identical make and model that was operated by the local commuter carrier, Cochise Airlines.

My plan was coming together.

I became a better pilot because of my teaching experience, even though I complained about it at the time. By sharing knowledge and reinforcing concepts with those you teach, you also learn and grow in the process.

CHAPTER 10

YOU HAVE TO START SOMEWHERE

It's a good idea to begin at the bottom in everything
except in learning to swim.

—Anonymous

The local, regional air carrier in Tucson, Arizona, where I went
to college, was Cochise Airlines, named after the fierce Native
American Apache chief of the Chiricahua Tribe. The warrior was
known for his fearless and relentless battle against armies and
settlers; the carrier was known for its fearless and relentless battle against regional and major airlines. Unlike Cochise, who died
privately on a reservation in 1874, Cochise Airlines would expire
very publicly on the steps of the bankruptcy courthouse in 1982.

I was in the no-man's land between that entry-level job of
flight instructing and a gig with the major airlines. In this career
limbo, the goal was to get a job flying as many hours as possible,
as fast as possible, in as big a plane as possible, to be qualified for
the big time. That path is often through the regional airlines, and
mine was through Cochise.

Everyone has their Cochise—a place where they pay their
dues on the way to greater things in the career of their dreams.

It's like a rite of passage, and it seems that the more heinous the indignities you suffer, the more bountiful the benefits you reap at the end of your trial. Well, almost.

Passengers coined many nicknames for the airline that became my rite of passage. "Go Cheap" Airlines reflected the low-cost nature of the operation. "Grilled Cheese" Airlines was descriptive of how some passengers felt after a summertime flight across the Arizona desert in the largely non–air-conditioned fleet. It was also known as "Oh Jeez" Airlines, after a phrase often uttered by nervous passengers at the start of the takeoff roll.

Cochise Airlines was my ticket to the big time. I figured I would graduate from college and go from my flying job at AFA to being a pilot for Cochise. There I'd be able to accumulate a lot of experience in a short period because Cochise was known for flying the hell out of its pilots. Although that doesn't sound good to me now, it sure did back then.

My strategy was to get to know everyone at the airline while I was still flight instructing and going to college. The Cochise operations hangar was conveniently located about 100 yards from my flight school. The hangar included training rooms, maintenance, a reservations office, and most importantly, the chief pilot's office.

Specifically, I would try to get hired now at the lowest-level job they had: a part-time customer service agent. This would allow me to continue school and teach flying, giving me access to the hangar and putting me in frequent and close proximity to the chief pilot, the guy who hired the flight crews.

I applied as a ticket agent, interviewed, and was swiftly hired to work a couple of flights a week. I was hired not due to any particular talent or aptitude but because the pay was so low that most of the people who applied could not get a job as a barker at a carnival.

Training was fast and furious. I was paired with an experienced agent named Byron, who was known for the speedy execution of his duties. He was a young college dropout in constant motion, which probably accounted for his very slim build despite consuming thousands of calories a day.

He had an in-depth knowledge of the airline business, which he exploited for his own selfish reasons. No matter the question, he had the answer. My most basic one was this: "Why is the two-letter airline code for Cochise Airlines the letters DP? Why isn't it CO?"

"Well," Byron said, "we asked for CO, but that was taken by Continental Airlines. So they just used the next letters in the alphabet, hence DP."

After dispatching the 9:00 a.m. flight to Phoenix, we would go to the donut shop at Tucson International Airport and have our coffee. Byron could quickly polish off a half dozen glazed crullers, wash them down with a large mocha, and then immediately start talking about lunch.

The one perk he loved most about his job was his cheap travel privileges. Although we flew little nine-passenger Cessna 402s in Arizona, somehow our company had negotiated agreements that allowed us cut-rate access to seats on the big airlines to just about anywhere in the world, with one caveat: there had to be empty seats.

I was soon released by Byron to work my flights by myself. Days later, Byron was released by Cochise Airlines.

Like Cochise the warrior, Byron had been conducting his own version of the sneak attack. To improve his chances of being boarded on other airlines, Byron would sit in the reservations office, pull some names out of the phone book, and reserve seats for dozens of fictitious passengers on flights to his intended vacation destination. When he checked in for the flight, the bogus passengers would not, leaving plenty of empty seats, and Byron would be off to Cancun in first class for about $37.

Still, Byron taught me well, so in his memory, and in honor of his speedy and knowledgeable execution, allow me to explain the process for working a flight by yourself.

Thirty minutes before departure time, you show up at the ticket counter, comfortably cool, and check in the passengers, tag their bags, and put them on the bag belt to send downstairs to the bag room. About 15 minutes before departure, you put a sign on the ticket counter directing any stragglers to the gate.

Running down the concourse, you flash your cheaply made ID badge at security and sprint out to the ramp to meet the arrival. As you open the terminal door, the hot air engulfs you as though you are downwind from a blazing wildfire.

Your first task on the ramp is to guide the incoming twin-engine prop plane to the parking spot, keeping a safe distance until the body choppers (I mean propellers) are stopped. From there, you open the door and guide the arriving passengers into the terminal.

The passengers file off the plane, often handing you small warm bags of vomit, which are particularly fetid in the torrid heat. You grudgingly accept them with two fingers, extend your arm as far as you can from your nose, and drop them into the ramp trash barrel.

Because it is a budget operation, the baggage cart is a dented, rusty brown VW bus with bald tires and no side door. In you jump, and you drive to the nose baggage compartment to yank the bags off the plane and onto the floor of the VW. From there, it is down the ramp to the baggage belt, screeching around every corner on your slicks. You deposit the inbound bags and retrieve the ones you just tagged upstairs, drive back up the ramp, and load them into the nose compartment.

Did I mention that this was Arizona, where the temperature can skyrocket into the triple digits? This mild exertion causes large crescents of perspiration to penetrate your shirt's armpits, and moist pellets form on your forehead, grow into droplets, overcome surface tension, and burst suddenly, streaming salty rivulets of sweat down your face.

Time to fuel the plane.

As you jump into the fuel truck, your entire back is soaked, and you stick sloppily to the vinyl seat back as you drive over to the nose of the plane. Ask the pilot how much gas he wants, attach the static wire from the fuel truck to the airplane (to ensure there will be no sparks, explosion, and fire), pump the gas into each fuel tank at the tip of the wing, unhook the static wire, and park the fuel truck.

Phew. But not done yet.

You now invite the outbound passengers to board. Many are regulars and notice how many bags of vomit came off the plane—a darn good indication of the turbulence level that day. They look at you with sympathy because by now you look like a contender in a wet T-shirt contest, soaked through and through.

Last but not least, you fill out the load sheet for the pilot, sweat dripping from the tips of your hair onto the paperwork, and hand it through the front window, knowing this will soon be over.

With a swift grab of the load sheet, you ensure that the cargo and passenger doors are closed, and you give the pilot the "okay to start" signal. You guide the plane away, and as it turns, you are blasted by hot air, pebbles, dust, and tart-smelling engine exhaust.

Time to break for the door to the terminal, jerk it open, duck inside, and slam it behind you like the airlock on the International Space Station. You turn, stop, exhale, lean against the wall, and take in the magnificent sting of that cold, dry, processed air.

Cruller time.

One day while retrieving some bags and cargo, I had an epiphany.

Long before everything went digital, doctors routinely shipped X-rays from city to city. One day, while in the baggage room, I retrieved one of these boxes, only to find that the heavy-metal container was badly twisted and mangled, almost as if it had been run over repeatedly by a baggage cart.

On the front of the box was a placard that read, "Caution—X-rays—WILL NOT BEND," onto which some smart-aleck airline person had written, "YES, THEY WILL."

I had found my people.

It wasn't a glamorous job, but it got my foot in the door and was worth every bead of sweat. Whether you start in the mailroom or as an intern or apprentice to someone you aspire to be, think of Cochise. Everyone pays their dues.

CHAPTER 11

DO THE RIGHT THING

Always do right. This will gratify some people and astonish the rest.

—Mark Twain

On the same day I graduated from college, I walked over to the Cochise operations hangar and handed my résumé and logbooks to the chief pilot, J. D. Brown.

J.D. was a former air force fighter pilot. He had a direct manner and Southern drawl that made you like him immediately. He was quietly religious and never wore it on his sleeve. Everyone respected him for his experience, flying skill, superior judgment, and leadership. He would never ask you to do something he wouldn't do himself.

One evening, a line of thunderstorms scored the sky between Tucson and Ft. Huachuca. It was getting dark, and the southern horizon from Tucson was black except for the frequent and spectacular lightning strikes. J.D. told the pilot he would fly the segments for him. When the pilot suggested they cancel, J.D. said no.

"You know what Mark Twain said? 'The trouble ain't that there is too many fools, but that the lightning ain't distributed right.' I'm no fool, so I will be just fine."

Whether it was his faith, skill, or luck, he made it down and back without incident. Most admirably, he ran a safe and legal operation. The worst thing for your career would be to get a violation from the FAA because you worked for a shoddy operator, and there were many of them.

J.D. knew me from my time working as a ticket agent and remembered how much I loved flying. What I lacked in experience, I made up for in enthusiasm. Unfortunately for me, although I was technically an adult, I looked about four years younger than I was. Nevertheless, he took a chance on me.

"You know, Steve, I can't put you in the scheduled operation just now, but I do have another flying job you may be interested in," he said.

"I'll take it," I said without hesitation.

"Well, before you say yes, hear me out. We have an air ambulance contract, and we need a pilot to be on call 24/7," he said. "We fly mostly preemies from around the state to the hospital here in Tucson, but on Friday or Saturday night you may get a good car crash or two after the bars close."

I was ecstatic to have a semi-steady job flying a multiengine airplane and the possibility of flying for the scheduled airline down the road.

"I'm in. Thanks, J.D.!"

"Okay, somebody will call you," he said and shook my hand.

A few days later, I was in training. We used a Cessna 421, owned by the pest-control company Truly Nolen and leased to Cochise when Nolen wasn't using it. Unlike the pest control trucks, the plane was not yellow and did not sport mouse ears; it was just white with green trim. It was basically a Cessna 402 that was pressurized and air-conditioned, with bigger engines.

Training was a breeze since I was already familiar with the Cessna 402, and upon completion, I was handed a beeper the size and weight of a brick patio paver. The interesting thing about the air ambulance job was that during the day my pager was as dead as tumbleweed. Late in the evening, however, it buzzed to life, and every call seemed to come between 9:00 p.m. and 3:00 a.m.

I usually flew around with a nurse, doctor, and one patient with a serious affliction. Sometimes the patients were preemies, and I once flew a child who weighed only one pound. The other part of the job J.D. didn't tell me about was cleaning up the blood in the airplane, which was a common by-product of a bad car crash or other serious accident. Back then, nobody worried too much about blood-borne pathogens, so you did the best you could with bleach and paper towels.

We flew in and out of remote airports in the mountains and deserts of Arizona. It was tough emotionally, and the late-night hours took their toll. Although the flying was fun for about a month, I soon longed for the consistency and sleep afforded to the pilots who flew the regular schedule.

Fortunately for me, the airline was in a growth spurt. It was about to augment the fleet of Cessna 402s with three brand-new Metro II aircraft, a 19-seat turboprop built by Swearingen in Texas. It was nicknamed the "San Antonio Sewer Pipe" due to its origin and the fact that it had a long and very narrow fuselage. Once those aircraft started to arrive, the senior pilots checked out on the new plane, creating slots for neophytes like me in the Cessna 402. However noble, I was done carrying around sick and injured people in the wee hours of the morning.

Flying the Cessna 402 was fun. The plane was a workhorse, and after a few months of long days with eight or nine landings, I got pretty good at flying it. I became a workhorse, too, because there was no first officer to help with the flying and no autopilot. I flew by hand, every second, and it was up to me alone to make sure things went well. At the end of a long day, I would no longer strive for the perfect touchdown. I was so tired from the heat and turbulence that I just wanted to get it safely on the ground.

These airplanes were flown hard. One of them developed an uncontrollable engine fire halfway between Prescott and Lake Havasu City, Arizona. Fortunately, it was daylight, and the pilot landed on a dirt road in the middle of the desert, and nobody got hurt. There was little left of the airplane as the fire consumed it. That incident got me thinking about what I would have done had it happened to me, at night, over terrain that was uninhabited and pitch black. The morbid joke was this: set up for an emergency landing in the desert, get down nice and low, and turn on the landing lights. If you don't like what you see, turn them off.

I can remember cruising in that same area in the inky darkness, looking down at the engine vents. At night the turbochargers glowed orange, which was a normal condition. It made me realize how close I was to being on fire all the time.

Another disturbing occurrence involved a very old airplane with more hours of flight time than any other Cessna 402 we knew of. Out of nowhere, it started making disconcerting cracking sounds that emanated from the main wing spar during turbulence. Our maintenance people couldn't find anything wrong with it. One night I flew it, and it made those same ominous sounds. I told J.D. about it, and I would be the last Cochise pilot to fly that airplane until they got to the bottom of it. Once again, J.D. made sure nothing bad happened on his watch.

Cessna took an interest in the 402 because it had been flown more hours than the manufacturer ever thought possible. These planes were designed as corporate shuttles, not airliners.

J.D. alerted Cessna, and they sent a test pilot to Arizona to fly it back to the factory in Wichita for further testing. On his departure day, he arrived ready to go—wearing a parachute.

The airplane was returned a few weeks later. I'm not sure what they did, but the only visible proof of a structural reinforcement was two metal strips riveted to the bottom of the wings. This was their way of reversing thousands of hours of abuse. It was Cessna's version of an aeronautical fountain of youth. Whatever they did, it stopped that infernal cracking noise, and the sturdy Cessna flew on.

Inside the Cessna, you were close to the passengers. In fact, one usually sat next to you. Since I looked like I was about 17 years old, I heard every wisecrack in the book.

"Are you old enough to have a driver's license?"

"Does your mother know you are here?"

"Timmy, where's Lassie?"

One woman even came up to me, squeezed my cheek, and said, "You look just like my grandson."

Another lady asked me, "Did you shave?"

"You mean this morning?" I asked.

"No," she replied. "Ever."

Just like during flight instruction, the summer afternoons were brutal. By noon the uneven heating of the scorched desert floor created fulminating shafts of rising air that pummeled you. The lower you were, the hotter it was, and the worse the turbulence. Most of our flight segments were about 45 minutes long, so as soon as we would get above the bumps into relatively cool and smooth air, it would be time to descend into the heat again.

Being the new guy, I got the hot, bumpy afternoon shift. We pilots prayed that we wouldn't get a "bagger," what we called an airsick passenger. As bad as that was, once one person got sick, everyone followed. The worst thing possible was a "nine-bagger," where everyone except you gets sick. The overpowering odor was almost enough to cause a "10-bagger," but I managed to avoid the embarrassment of puking in front of my passengers.

Cochise was a shoestring operation, and no city illustrated that more than the overnight in Kingman, Arizona. Kingman was a subsidy city, meaning the airline got paid to fly there even if there were no passengers, and there usually weren't any.

Most of the afternoon was spent flying from Tucson to Fort Huachuca, back to Tucson, then up to Phoenix, Lake Havasu, and finally Kingman. Kingman at night was what's known as a black-hole approach. There were mountains all around it and no approach procedure to provide glide path information. You just had to eyeball it. The runway looked like a tiny glowing postage stamp dancing in a sea of blackness.

Once on the ground, you'd get into the crew car, which was an ancient 1961 Chevy Impala. It had about 300,000 miles on it and bad tires, and you prayed there was gas in it because if there wasn't, you had to buy it on your meager salary. And it took weeks to get reimbursed from the financially struggling company.

The next stop was the crew hotel, which was not a hotel at all but a ratty rented condo. They told us there was maid service every day, but there was little evidence of that. The best food in town was Kentucky Fried Chicken, where you would stop to order dinner. Then you'd head to the local 7-Eleven to buy a beer or two.

By the time the new Metroliners came on the line in quick succession, I was very interested. The aircraft was flown with two pilots. Even though I'd be a first officer instead of a captain, I was happy to leave the single-pilot Cessna operation behind and get the chance to fly an airplane with turbine engines. It was an opportunity I couldn't turn down. Like the airliners I longed to fly, these new airplanes were air-conditioned.

I saw the first new Metroliner taxiing up to our hangar at Tucson International Airport, fresh from the factory. It emitted the distinctive piercing whine of its turbine engines, and the whiff of jet exhaust smelled like opportunity to any aspiring airline pilot. The fuselage hue was supposed to be tan, like the desert, but it looked more like a weird flesh color, with brown and orange stripes along the side. I once heard an air traffic controller at Los Angeles International Airport point us out to another aircraft in that manner.

"American 332, do you see the Cochise Airlines Metroliner at your 12 o'clock position and four miles?"

"Ah, we're looking," said the American pilot.

"It's down low. It's the color of a Band-Aid."

"Oh yeah. Got it in sight."

Even with the weird color, there was nothing like a shiny new airplane. True to its Arizona heritage, the number on its side was N23AZ.

Shortly after landing, the door opened, and a few of us piled into the empty cabin, taking in that new airplane smell. At that point we didn't know who would get to fly the new toy, and operating it had its pros and cons.

The pros were that it was a turbine-powered airplane with two engines, which provided excellent experience that would make us more competitive for a job with the big airlines. Unlike the Cessna, it was pressurized, so it could fly higher and farther away from the bumpy air down below. And it was air-conditioned, helping pilots avoid the dehydration that was common in the Cessna. Best of all, it flew a lot faster.

The cons were that it was an incredibly uncomfortable airplane with a short, stubby wing that made you feel every bump, like driving a BMW with low-profile tires over a dirt road. It was also terribly noisy, with the whirling tips of its big propellers within inches of the fuselage and right behind the cockpit. You didn't just wear a headset when you flew it, you'd put in earplugs and then put the headset over them.

It also had a design flaw. When the landing gear was down, the doors on the main landing gear were oriented 90 degrees to the slipstream—that is, they acted like little metal parachutes that slowed you down. They were helpful if you were high and fast and trying to descend, but in case of an engine failure on takeoff, they were your enemy. Under most conditions, the airplane would not climb on one engine if the landing gear was down. If you lost an engine on takeoff, before the gear retracted, the remaining engine would take you to the scene of the accident. You couldn't climb in that condition.

The Metroliner engineers came up with a novel solution. They installed a solid-fuel rocket in the airplane's tail. That way, if an engine failed on takeoff, you would just ignite the rocket, which allegedly would give you enough of a push to climb on one engine while you waited for the gear to retract. Once the gear retracted, it flew fine on one engine.

In theory, this all sounded pretty good, and no one I know ever had to try this maneuver. Even so, like the carton of milk in your refrigerator, these rockets had an expiration date. Beyond that time you were no longer guaranteed that they would function properly.

With encouragement from our maintenance folks, one of our crews decided to try an experiment with one of the expired rockets. They took off, got to a safe altitude, and fired the rocket. When they returned, I asked the pilot how it went.

"Well, you felt the deceleration when it stopped more than you felt the acceleration when it started," he said. "I'm not sure it would do what it was supposed to do. It could just end up igniting the post-crash wreckage," he said with a chuckle.

But despite all these drawbacks, the fact that the big airlines liked the turbine multi-engine experience trumped everything. I would be an idiot to turn down the new position.

I quickly qualified as a first officer on the Metroliner. A few weeks later, we took delivery of two more of them, and I soon found myself a captain again, this time in the turboprop.

With more airplanes, our route structure expanded. Soon we were flying to places like San Diego and Los Angeles. It was a great experience, and we felt like we were rubbing shoulders with the big guys. As swift as they were, our planes flew a lot slower than the jets. Air traffic controllers were very familiar with the Metroliner's capabilities and were always asking us to go fast to keep from being an airborne "speed bump" for the jets. They are typically assigned a speed of 250 knots until close to the airport.

These knowledgeable controllers knew that our maximum speed was 249 knots. You'd hear them say, "United 985, maintain 250 knots until a seven-mile final." Then they'd say, "Cochise 395, maintain 249 knots until a seven-mile final."

I thought I was doing a pretty good job for the airline and once received a kudos letter from the president of the company. In it, he detailed whatever it was that I did, then closed by writing, "You have set an example to which we can all *expire*" instead of *"aspire."*

That was more foreshadowing than he would ever know because about three years later, the airline did "expire"... in bankruptcy court.

Even with the malapropism, I had achieved my goal. Guided by J.D.'s leadership and integrity I had built a strong reputation and stayed out of hot water with the FAA.

My next stop would be with a major airline.

Chapter 12

@&#% the Cat—Foster Your Curiosity

A wise man can learn more from a foolish question
than a fool can learn from a wise answer.

—Bruce Lee

You've heard phrases like "continuous improvement" and "continuing education." They refer to this simple truth. If you don't keep trying and learning new things throughout your life and career, you will become a bore, lose at trivia, and get passed over for promotions by less qualified peers. I exaggerate, but you get the point. It takes a lot of work to make a dream come true.

Going from a regional carrier to a major airline is like getting called up from the Toledo Mud Hens to the Detroit Tigers. It's a pilot's dream.

With that goal in mind, I took my wannabe airline pilot Jerry Toci's advice and did something every day to get hired by the big airlines. I submitted applications to every carrier and regularly updated them. They had hired few pilots in years, so I was elated when, after a few years of trying, I received a letter from United Airlines.

I immediately did everything I could to prepare for my shot at the big time, including securing the aid of an airline pilot interview prep company. With experience across all the major carriers, they shared common interview questions and other critical information so that you approached your interview feeling better prepared. Just taking the initiative improved my confidence level. Knowing your subject well will make you feel more confident and at ease, and the interviewers will appreciate that you've become a student of their business.

Since this was before the internet became commonplace, I went to the library to research United Airlines and prepare a few questions. I knew that at the end of the interview, they would ask me if I had any questions. I heard that United was known to ask technical questions about the airplane you were currently flying, so I spent hours studying my flight manual. Feeling that the airline gods were watching, the more I prepared, the better I felt.

With my mind in sharp focus, I turned my attention to my attire. I bought the standard blue suit, red tie, and black shoes, and got the obligatory haircut off the ears and collar. Hearing that high cholesterol can knock you out of the running, I even began to monitor what I ate.

I arrived in Los Angeles the day before the interview and stayed at the airport Marriott hotel. I wanted to be on time and well rested for the battery of psychological, knowledge, and logic tests I would take before the actual interview. The preparation paid off—everything went smoothly. I left feeling confident and optimistic.

A week later I received a letter from United stating that my application was "deferred," which meant I was neither accepted nor rejected but that I would be considered again in the future. Bummed to be stranded in hiring limbo, I took my disappointment and new haircut back to Cochise Airlines. I continued to fly as many hours as I could, updating my application as I gained more experience.

Several months later I received another letter from United. This time I was to report to the United Airlines Flight Training Center in Denver for "further processing." I was psyched. They hadn't forgotten about me after all. I repeated my thorough preparation, got another haircut, reassembled my interview uniform, and flew to Denver. Following another battery of tests and yet another interview, I was given a physical exam by the company doctor.

Looking around at my competition, I was disheartened—I was one of the youngest pilots in the group. Maybe it was my insecurity, but they all looked more experienced than me.

While waiting for my blood test, I chatted with an air force pilot who was flying KC-135s, the military version of the four-engine B707 transport, used to refuel other aircraft.

"Yeah, I got this in the bag. A couple of guys from my unit already got hired. How much jet time you got?" he asked.

"Uh, none. I fly a turboprop."

"A weed eater, huh?" He looked me up and down and just shook his head. "Well, good luck, then."

I don't know what that guy bagged, but I never saw him again.

A few more weeks passed, and I was getting exasperated. This was the biggest opportunity of my career, and it felt like nothing was happening.

Finally, right before Christmas, my phone rang. "We'd like to offer you a job as a United Airlines Flight Officer."

I couldn't believe it. All my research, memorization, dietary abstinence, personal grooming, and other preparation had paid off. I immediately said yes, was congratulated, and then was

given a class date to report to the same place I'd done my interview, the United Airlines Flight Training Center.

My learning adventure continued in Denver's frigid cli-
mate, where I spent the coldest day of the year. I reported for my
first day of training to see 12 other excited but nervous airmen
there, all with identical haircuts. Initial training lasted a few
weeks, and we all breezed through it.

Although we were all pilots, in our entry-level status, we
would not fly at all. We'd be the third person in the cockpit,
known as the flight engineer. We did the preflight walk-around
inspection, computed the aircraft performance, and monitored
the aircraft systems from a large panel in the back of the cockpit,
ensuring fuel was going to the engines, the cabin temperature
was comfortable, and the other aircraft systems were running
properly. All the newer airplanes eliminated this position, replac-
ing the flight engineer with automation, except for the walk-
around inspection. A computer still can't quite do that.

The big question in our minds was our initial assignment.
Where would we be based, and what airplane would the airline
assign to us? Being the youngest guy in the class meant I got
whatever assignments were left over, and I was awarded a JFK
DC-8 flight engineer position. Most of my new-hire colleagues
lived on the West Coast, and the DC-8 was known as a somewhat
complicated and challenging airplane compared to the smaller
B737 or B727. To make matters worse, United had about a half
dozen different models of the DC-8, and you had to know all the
many differences between them. My classmates were happy to
forego the big four-engine plane.

When the first airplane was delivered to United in 1959,
the DC-8 was known as the queen of the fleet. It was the largest
airplane at United Airlines until the DC-10 and B747 were developed years later. It was long and skinny, with four big engines,

and flew the choice long-haul routes, including Hawaii. It was known for being tank-like in its construction, and the outside of it looked like it had more rivets than a German U-boat. Instead of electro-mechanical actuators found in newer planes, the DC-8 was controlled by a network of thick cables that ran throughout the airplane. They were reliable, but they were also heavy and made controlling the plane feel like flying a half-filled swimming pool.

Its complexity worried me a little because I believe there are two types of people in the world. "Home Depot" people and "Office Depot" people. Home Depot people grew up with Legos and erector sets. They built go-karts, tuned up their own cars, and could take engines apart and put them back together again. They owned ham radios that they built from kits. These were hands-on types, with dirty fingernails, do-it-yourselfers who had tremendous mechanical aptitude. They obviously learned from doing, able to follow complicated instructions.

Then there are Office Depot people. These people don't fix things themselves; they call on a Home Depot person to do it for them. They could fill a car with gas and mow a lawn, but that is about it. They grew up fooling with computers, slide projectors, and calculators and didn't handle anything greasy. Some of them turned out to be the AV guy at your high school. While generally good with paper, they have a bit of trouble with schematics and anything three-dimensional.

I am an Office Depot guy, so that's why I was worried.

I struggle to hold my own with any type of technical detail. I vaguely know the difference between a volt and an amp, and I have trouble distinguishing between a diode and a geode. A hydraulic system schematic looks to me like a map of the New York City subway system. Although fascinated by airplanes, I'm more interested in knowing how to operate them, not the details of how they operate.

So I felt more than a little trepidation at my impending DC-8 class, especially since the curriculum was very much focused on the technical details of the airplane.

Having completed indoctrination training, I warily walked into the DC-8 ground school classroom on day one. The back of the room was filled with giant training contraptions on wheels that were used to teach how the major systems on the airplane worked: fuel, hydraulics, pneumatics, etc. My heart sank.

I looked around the room and realized I was the only new-hire pilot in the class. Furthermore, everyone else in the class—captains, first officers, and other flight engineers—had all been through the school in years past. Cutbacks forced them temporarily to fly smaller and lower paid aircraft, and now that the airline was growing again, they were back on the old DC-8. This was an initial training course for me but just a refresher for them.

This was not going to be easy.

The instructor tore through the course at breakneck speed. Unlike me, the other students didn't need to spend a lot of time studying, since this entire class was just a review of what they had already learned.

The instructor would preface every new topic as follows: "Okay, you all know this..." and would move through each subject quicker than you could digest a bad Tijuana street taco.

Despite my protestations, I was not allowed to ask many questions, as each one would delay quitting time and thus the other pilots' daily appointment at the hotel bar. I didn't even have the chance to ask a foolish question.

Having flown many different types of aircraft gave me the foundation for getting through school, but I had to spend many hours alone, studying the complicated systems and procedures and solving tedious performance computations. We were issued a lengthy handout of problems, and I managed to solve every single one. Thank goodness they provided the answers so I could back into the solution.

Once I completed ground school, it was time for the flight simulator. Since I had never been a flight engineer, it was hard to adjust my mindset. Usually, when the pilots are busy, the flight engineer isn't. And when the flight engineer is occupied, the pilots aren't. I managed to muddle my way through the course, and my instructor informed me that I was ready for my oral exam and flight simulator check ride.

The stakes were high. I was betting my career on the outcome of this testing. It was possible to fail and get another chance, but nobody wanted to take that risk.

The day before the check rides, we learned who would be administering them. Our instructor took a poll.

"Bill, who did you get?"

"Johnson."

"Yeah, he's good. Likes to ask about the hydraulic system."

"Tom, who did you draw?"

"Dixon."

"He likes the electrical system. Steve, who'd you get?"

"Masonheimer."

There was a long pause, and my instructor gave me a worried look, and then moved on.

"Rick, who'd you get?"

That made me nervous. It turns out that Masonheimer had a particularly surly manner, which I learned the next day.

We met in the briefing room. Masonheimer wore a suit and tie, as did I, and was as grave and somber as an undertaker.

He gave me a desultory handshake, checked my paperwork, and dove into the oral exam.

The briefing room was equipped with detailed photos of all the control panels in the cockpit. Masonheimer started at the top left corner of the flight engineer's panel and asked me questions about every light and switch, and there were a lot of them. Since I was going to be a flight engineer, I figured I should focus my study on my panel. I had over prepared and managed to answer every question about the switches and dials correctly.

Unable to stump me, Masonheimer then did something rather unusual. He started to ask me about all the lights and switches on the forward panel, topics usually reserved for the pilots. I did well until he got to the landing gear lights.

"So what happens if you manually open the gear door from down by the wheel? Will this door light be on or off?"

I was stumped. I had no idea but had a fifty-fifty chance.

I guessed wrong.

Masonheimer launched into a discussion of how important that light is and how someone could be injured if the door suddenly snapped closed.

I honestly believe that if I'd gotten an answer wrong sooner, the exam might have ended sooner.

We then headed to the flight simulator. It was flown by a captain and first officer "fill-in." Their job was to do only what was required and not lead me or help me too much.

On the first takeoff, Masonheimer failed an engine, and the captain appropriately aborted the takeoff.

I sprang into action, monitoring engine reverse, ensuring the equipment cooling switch went to ground mode, etc.

We came to a halt. Masonheimer looked at me.

"Open the simulator door," he said.

"Huh?"

"Open the simulator door," he said again.

I opened the door and was staring at the back wall of the simulator bay.

"What do you see?"

"Nothing," I said.

"That's right. You forgot to make a PA announcement telling everyone to stay in their seats, so they all panicked and evacuated the plane unnecessarily."

I understood his point, but I thought there might have been a less sarcastic way of illustrating it.

We managed to go through all the check ride requirements in about an hour. When we were done, I packed up my flight kit and headed to the briefing room. I still didn't know if I'd passed.

Masonheimer sat down and consulted his notes.

"Okay, I'll give you an 85 out of 100. But we don't learn anything by talking about what you did right, so let's discuss what you did wrong."

He then carefully reviewed every element of the check ride, signed my paperwork, and I was done.

"Satisfactory."

I wanted a water-cannon salute, fireworks, at least a marching band. After all I had been through, I was happy to cling to that one little word: satisfactory. With it, I was now past the biggest hurdle to becoming a fully qualified flight officer. And my education was just beginning.

At United Airlines I worked hard and progressed over the years, rising from line pilot through a series of management jobs. I earned an MBA and eventually became the senior vice president of Flight Operations and director of Operations. But I am most proud of being a pilot.

Whatever arc your career trajectory takes, remember there will be many opportunities along the way to learn. You will gain insight from successes and from failures—from your own as well as those of your colleagues. Just keep learning, growing, and finding ways to raise your personal bar.

CHAPTER 13

SYMPHONY ON DECK

True, there is no "I" in team, but there is a "U" in suck.

—Anonymous

When you have confidence in your own skills, it can be hard to allow others to take over. Even so, pursuing a dream is not a solo effort. Sometimes, delegating and sharing your load is not only more efficient but also creates opportunities for innovation and creativity. I thought I knew a thing or two about teamwork. I learned otherwise, years later in my professional career, when I spent two days aboard the aircraft carrier USS *Abraham Lincoln*.

Although it was part of a two-day employer appreciation day junket, they had me at "aircraft carrier." I would be joined on this short cruise by a diverse group of passengers, which included pilots, airline managers, former military officers, teachers, and high school counselors. At first, I couldn't determine what we all had in common. Then it hit me. We were all in a position to persuade young people to join the US Navy. This wasn't an appreciation day as much as training to be unwitting navy recruiters.

Focusing on my own excitement, I shamelessly joined my fellow passengers, including Charlie Maynard, an airline pilot and former navy F-18 fighter pilot, when we rendezvoused at the naval air station on North Island in San Diego. From there, we would hitch a plane ride to the carrier. After check-in and a brief introduction, we received a helmet, goggles, ear protection, and a life jacket. No one had the heart to tell us that, in our civilian clothes wearing the protective gear, we looked like a bunch of landlubber bobblehead dolls.

We walked out of the briefing building to board the airplane that would take us to the carrier, which was steaming about 50 miles offshore. It was a Grumman C-2 Greyhound, a twin-engine high-wing cargo aircraft designed to carry supplies and people to and from aircraft carriers for the US Navy. Nicknamed the COD (carrier onboard delivery), it was a critical part of naval logistics support.

A sturdy airplane, it was built for many things. However, passenger comfort was not one of them. In fact, it was so boxy that it looked like the Grumman had been left in its delivery crate, with just the wings and tail sticking out. Everything on it had been compressed, and the large flat black nose gave the front of the airplane the appearance of a koala.

Instead of entering through a door, we walked up a gaping ramp that opened into the back of the airplane, which I heard a few of my fellow passengers compare to walking the plank. Inside were 26 passenger seats, but they all faced aft, or backward, which was disorienting.

The rear door slowly closed, leaving us sitting strapped in semidarkness. There were two tiny windows at the rear of the cabin, too high to see out of, so it was impossible to tell where we were going. This must've been what it was like to be in a large space capsule.

The sidewalls were metal, with the insulation showing through. There were no flight attendants, no predeparture refreshments, no greeting from the captain, no entertainment, no pillow, and no blanket. This was utilitarian flying at its best. I had a sudden appreciation for the soldiers who traveled this way all the time.

What should have been a 10-minute flight went on for over a half hour. We climbed, leveled off, and turned this way and that until I was totally lost. Tension built. We looked at each other, trying to predict when we would slam onto the deck of the ship, hook an arresting cable, and come to a screeching halt. Or miss the cable and topple off the deck.

All this time I was imagining what landing would feel like. I presumed the deceleration shouldn't be too bad as long as we had our heads pressed against the headrests. If not, the force of the deceleration would do that for us automatically.

Finally, our only hint of an imminent landing was the feeling that the pilot was making a lot of very small, abrupt control inputs and then—BAM, we were on the deck.

After a brief taxi, the engines shut down, and the rear entryway slowly opened. The brilliant sun temporarily blinded us. The activity outside was furious. Jets launching, sailors in different-colored shirts scuttling everywhere, firefighters lugging equipment along the side of the deck. Exiting the plane, we walked the plank in reverse, across the deck and down into the guts of the ship.

We were guided back up to the flight deck. Standing there, we watched the experienced teams practice the process of launch and recovery. It was the most amazing display of teamwork I've ever seen, in such an incredibly challenging environment.

There were all types of aircraft: COD transports, F-18 Hornet fighters, EA-18G Growlers for electronic warfare, E-2C Hawkeyes for airborne early warning (AEW), and a variety of helicopters used for antisubmarine protection and search and rescue.

On board the ship we were issued new protective safety gear. These required items included heavy-duty helmets called cranials that protected our brains from bumps and our hearing from the cacophony, goggles for eye protection, and life jackets just in case we got blown off the deck by jet blast and fell the roughly 60 feet into the ocean.

I was paired up with Charlie Maynard, whose naval experience included plenty of carrier landings. He wore his navy flight suit, and in it he displayed the natural confidence of a fighter jock. We walked to within 30 feet of the jets preparing for launch. A baffling array of people scurried around the deck, giving each other hand signals. Considering the noise from the constant takeoffs and landings, that was the most effective way to communicate. The apparent chaos was actually a well-choreographed symphony of activity.

Everyone on deck wore a different-colored shirt. White jerseys denoted air wing quality control personnel, plane inspectors, liquid oxygen crews, safety personnel, and medical personnel. Red indicated people who handled bombs and ordinance. Purple designated fuelers, or "the Grapes." Green was mostly deck personnel. Yellow for aircraft handling officers and plane directors; brown were aircraft plane captains; and blue were plane handlers, elevator operators, and tractor drivers. Together, they were as synchronized as an orchestra but working in a much more dangerous environment.

In front of us, a sailor hooked the nose wheel of an F-18 Hornet to the catapult in a slot on the deck. It would use nuclear reactor–generated steam to take the plane from zero to flying speed in just a few seconds.

The deck crew raised a jet blast deflector behind the plane, and when everyone was in position and all the final checks made, the catapult officer set the system based on the weight of the aircraft. The biggest fear was that the 19-year-old in charge might apply too little oomph and the plane would fail to reach flying speed and drop off the end of the deck to be unceremoniously run over by the ship.

When ready to launch, the pilot applied full power, held in place by something called a holdback fitting, which breaks when the catapult activates. The pilot gave a salute, and then did the first thing that totally baffled me: he took his right hand off the controls and grabbed one of the handles on the window frame.

Charlie later explained that the F-18 is so advanced that the fly-by-wire flight controls would establish the exact optimum attitude to ensure a successful takeoff. If the pilot had his hand on the stick, the jolt of going from zero to 165 knots in about two seconds could inadvertently apply the wrong control inputs. The pilot does, however, quickly assume control a second after launch.

If everything goes well, the plane flies off into the horizon. If not, the pilot punches out, pulling the ejector handle and activating the ejection seat to escape before the plane hurdles into the ocean. Hopefully, the pilot floats down beside the ship to be picked up by one of the rescue helicopters standing by.

We watched a half dozen Hornets go through this perfectly choreographed procedure, one after another, with sailors rushing all over the deck. I was amazed that nobody was blown overboard, sucked into a jet inlet, skewered by the pointy nose of the planes, or whacked by the catapult. Obviously, their training, experience, and strict adherence to well-defined procedure kept this from becoming a catastrophe.

Next, we walked down the deck to watch the landing airplanes. Four parallel cables stretched across the deck, about 50 feet apart, comprised the landing area. The object of each arriving airplane was to hook one of them, ideally the number-two wire.

Like the catapult in reverse, the jets would approach the back of the ship at high speed and slam into the deck, doing the second thing that surprised me: adding full power as they touched down. That made no sense until I realized that if they missed hooking a cable, they'd need all that power to get back in the air for another try.

I was enjoying this immensely until Charlie leaned in and yelled over the deafening noise, "I was on the ship when one of the cables snapped. It cut a guy right in half, pretty much where you are standing." I looked at him skeptically, he nodded back at me solemnly, and I took a few involuntary steps backward. We were done here.

We toured the rest of the ship and were invited to join a small group of visitors for dinner with the ship's captain. About a dozen of us filed into the private dining area and were greeted by Captain Kendall Card. He was responsible for everything that happened aboard the ship, including ensuring the safety of the crew and passengers and, most importantly, the training and teamwork that we saw on deck.

While we were having dinner, Captain Card explained that the entire ship's crew would be performing a fire drill, simulating an explosion on board the ship. It was an example of the constant training the crew undergoes.

After dinner we were permitted to watch night carrier operations but not from deck level. The navy was risking a lot with us on the deck during the day, so they certainly weren't going to allow us on the blacked-out deck at night.

The entire spectacle was much more dramatic in the dark, with the exhaust from the full-throttled jets glowing white and the tail hooks kicking up a shower of sparks as they glanced off the deck like a giant Fourth of July sparkler. Night carrier landings are the most difficult for a navy pilot to master, as I was often told by my father.

We were permitted to visit the bridge, where Captain Card was intently watching everything. He had a cabin below deck and a small sleeping area right there on the bridge, where he stayed while the crew conducted flight operations. We later learned that when he was deployed during the Gulf War, he spent days on the bridge without leaving.

After retiring to our cabins under the flight deck that night, it was impossible to sleep. Every few minutes a plane took off or landed, and it was as though the kitchen crew was banging 14 pots together in the galley. Mercifully, the noise ceased at midnight when air operations were completed, and we were finally able to get some sleep. I imagined the sailors who had to put up with this all the time got used to the racket, but I sure didn't.

We arose early the next morning, ate breakfast in the sailors' mess, and toured the ship. We saw just a fraction of the thousands of people it took to operate this floating city, everyone from officers and fighter pilots to sailors who were constantly and obsessively cleaning it. We toured the vast hangar deck, which housed many of the aircraft, and the tiny recesses in the bottom of the ship.

Toward the stern, we entered a small room with a lone sailor sitting on a stool, staring at a mechanical contraption that was connected to the ship's rudder. He was standing the "Aft Steering Watch" to take control of the rudder if the rudder commands from the helm failed. That's all he did during his four-hour watch: stare at the rudder. And yet, his job, like all the others, was vital to keeping the ship safe and running efficiently.

Later that day we experienced our own catapult shot from inside the COD that would transport us back to North Island. As before, we suited up, filed into the back of the plane, and took our rear-facing seats. The wings were folded as we boarded, and I hoped like hell they would remember to extend them before we took off.

"That can't happen, right? Take off with the wings folded?" I asked Charlie, who was next to me.

"Probably not," he said, not the least bit reassuringly.

I imagined the effect the massive acceleration would have on my head. Since we faced backward, we would have only our shoulder harnesses to restrain us during the painful acceleration, this time from zero to about 135 knots in two seconds.

As before, the loading ramp slowly closed, entombing us in our metal shell. I wondered how I would make it to the escape hatch if the catapult operator misjudged our weight and we plunged into the ocean. Could I get out before the ship ran over us and the massive propellers diced us into shark chum?

I heard the rumble of the starting engines and hoped they remembered to extend the wings. There would be a much shorter taxi out due to the very close confines of the ship's deck. We moved a bit and waited. I wished someone had given me a little notice before the launch.

"Make sure your shoulder straps are tight," Charlie said. "I once saw a guy—"

At that instant I felt the catapult shot. I was violently thrust forward against my shoulder harnesses. The weak elastic on my goggle strap pulled them a good inch off my face. My legs and arms flew out to the horizontal position, parallel to the floor. Everything was in slow motion, and it was physically painful. The seconds dragged on as the acceleration got more and more intense. I thought, "When is this going to end?"

Suddenly, it stopped. We were airborne. My legs and arms flopped to my sides, and my goggles snapped back against my face, albeit a little askew. I straightened them for the easy 15-minute flight to the base, where we made a welcomed and smooth landing.

In the officer's club downing a post-mission beer, Charlie explained to me that there were remarkably few casualties on the flight deck. It was all about training, discipline, leadership, and teamwork, from that guy staring at the rudder all the way to Captain Card. These men and women who worked day and night in breathtakingly difficult conditions performed with the precision of a world-class team.

When teams work together toward a common goal, individual accomplishments grow exponentially. There may be no "I" in team, but there is a "U" in outstanding.

Chapter 14

When Opportunity Beckons, Jump

If a window of opportunity appears, don't pull down the shade.

—Tom Peters

Most of the time, we must create our own opportunities, as difficult as that may be. Every now and then fate hovers like a hummingbird just out of the corner of your eye with a possible opportunity. It's there for a moment, and you need to grab it.

One such opportunity came my way when I was having lunch with my friend Dan Wolfe, founder of Wolfe Air Aviation. His company is the premier provider of high-end aerial photography for everything from research and development, to the military, to Hollywood's big screen. I told him I was fascinated by the movie business.

Out of nowhere, he said, "Well, goddamn it, Forte, why don't you come work for me part time?"

I'd never considered working for him, and I told him I knew nothing about being a movie pilot, but he was undeterred. "Hey, you are an experienced jet pilot, and we need good guys."

Dan often hired pilots to complement the formation pilots, so I was sold.

Dan is a great guy and has done a lot of favors for people in Hollywood and elsewhere over the years. He has a long list of stories about the business.

For example, in 1991 he got a call from his colleague Tak Fujimoto, director of photography on a film he had just completed with director Jonathan Demme. Tak described it to Dan as a "really good film."

"What's it about?" Dan asked.

"It's about a guy who eats people. It's called *The Silence of the Lambs*."

"Oh yeah, that sounds like it should do *really* well at the box office," Dan said sarcastically, which explains why Dan is not a movie critic.

Tak told Dan that the film was done, but after they started screening it, they realized they needed an aerial shot to help tie two scenes together. It is a critical shot toward the end of the movie where Clarice Starling (Jodie Foster) is on the phone to FBI agent Jack Crawford (Scott Glenn), who is on board a C-130, headed to where they thought the murderer was hiding. They had shots of the FBI getting on the C-130, inside the C-130, and getting off the C-130 but no in-flight shots that tied it together.

Orion Pictures was on the verge of bankruptcy and not willing to invest another dime in the movie. Tak asked how much it would cost to do a twilight aerial shot of a C-130. Dan said it would be about $40,000 plus the cost of the C-130. That was too much.

Fortunately, Dan already had the Learjet prepped for another job at Edwards AFB, with a crew on board, so when they finished that job, they flew down to Burbank to do the quick shot, saving them the charge for the prep and wrap.

When the tiny Learjet landed at Burbank, Tak and the director were waiting for it.

Tak took one look at the Learjet and said, "There is only one flaw in this plan, Dan. I'm not going up in that little thing!"

Demme said, "Look, I'm paying for this out of my own pocket, so I'll go."

Dan tried to dissuade him because the only remaining seat was in the front and faced sideways, which is not the optimal position to be in when the airplane starts pulling Gs during the various join-ups, pull-aways, and rejoins. "You will absolutely get sick," Dan told Demme.

"I don't care. I'm going," Demme said.

Dan handed him an airsick bag and said, "Welcome aboard!"

As predicted, the intrepid Mr. Demme got sick after the first harsh maneuver. Still, he deserved credit for going along despite a guaranteed miserable ride.

Although I was glad that Dan was confident in my abilities, the first step was to quickly take a course on how to fly the Learjet. I found a school in Dallas that was surprisingly affordable and signed up.

Learjet ground school consisted of five straight days in the classroom discussing how pilots have gotten killed in that flying bullet, usually by doing something stupid. Don, my instructor, had been around Learjets for about 30 years. He knew everything about them, inside and out, and instilled in us a respect for the airplane.

Every time we discussed a component of the airplane—electrical, pressurization, fuel, engines—he had a story about how a Learjet crashed due to a screw up. If he was trying to get my attention, it worked. Ground school devolved into a continuous stream of horror stories about how legions of pilots, and their passengers, met their end by doing sketchy things in the Learjet.

I was becoming increasingly nervous.

When we talked about the engines, Don had stories about engines failing and Learjets careening out of control. When we talked about the hydraulic system, he had stories about control failures and loss of control. It was amazing.

I tried to stump him. "How about tires? Anybody killed because of tires?" I asked like a smart aleck.

"In 2008, Columbia Metro Airport in South Carolina, Lear 60. Aborted takeoff. Four fatalities, two survivors," Don said. "The Safety Board said severely under-inflated tires were a causal factor. They couldn't stop."

A few incidents couldn't be blamed on the airplane. In 1983, a Lear 25 crashed on a night courier run. Both pilots had been "exposed" to marijuana and CO_2, which showed up on the post-accident blood tests. There was another in 1993 where the captain was under the influence of cocaine. All occupants were killed. The airplane is hard enough to fly sober. Flying it impaired was suicide.

Accidents also occurred when pilots got lost and flew into terrain, got high and fast on the approach and ran off the end of the runway, or simply ran out of fuel and crashed. There was even a long list of accidents that took place while training in the airplane—which was why I was glad that all my flight training would take place inside a flight simulator. At least I couldn't get killed in a simulator.

Or so I thought.

In 2014 a bizarre training accident occurred that made me forever a bit paranoid about training in a flight simulator. A *real* airplane crashed into a simulator building in Wichita, Kansas, killing the three men inside the simulator and the pilot of the aircraft. I guess when it's your time to go...

In the break room, I got the chance to hang out with the other corporate pilots, a world foreign to me. I soon learned that, like working at the airlines, it's all about the size of your... airplane. Bigger is better.

Since Learjets were the smallest planes, their pilots were the bottom of the general aviation food chain. Pay was mostly tied to the size of aircraft, so we were the bottom feeders. The real elite were the pilots who flew the Gulfstreams, recognized as the biggest and best corporate jets ever. I once asked a Gulfstream factory demo pilot how fast they flew. Did they fly at the optimum speed for economy?

He laughed in my face and said, "Hey, if you can afford $65 million for a jet, you fly as fast as that son of a bitch will go. To hell with the fuel bill."

The simulator was not exactly state of the art. The visual system was archaic, but somehow I managed to fill all the squares, yank and bank at the appropriate times, and pass my FAA check ride.

With the ink still wet on my new certificate, I called the producer, Beth, who was Dan's daughter, to announce that I was a fully qualified Learjet captain and ready to go to work.

Later that week I met Dan at Hawthorne Airport to check out the airplane. The Lear 25 was beautiful with a dark gray paint job and a red stripe down the side. It looked like it was going 1,000 miles an hour just sitting on the ramp. Under the left wing was a cylinder-shaped camera pod that looked ominously like the bomb that was on that military plane I saw fly over my house in 1962. On the bottom of the fuselage was a small periscope attached to the RED movie camera, which the cinematographer could point in a variety of directions.

For a typical shoot, the back of the plane is crammed with people and equipment. There can be as many as five people: a producer, director, movie camera operator, camera tech (assistant cameraman), and photographer who shot still photos. The movie camera takes up the bulk of the space. Only an articulating mirror in an external dome projects out of the bottom of the jet, gathering images through an optical relay.

The techs were usually young and dressed in shorts, T-shirts, and hiking boots. They did this for extra money in their spare time. Otherwise, they worked on feature films with Tom Cruise, Angelina Jolie, and other A-listers. They were all very low key and had a talent for fading into the background so that the stars barely knew they were there. Even so, like a 12-year-old girl in middle school, they heard all the celebrity gossip. I won't disclose what they said—I'm saving that for my lucrative call from the *National Enquirer.*

The Lear 25 was great for formation flying because the noisy old straight-jet engines responded more quickly to power changes than more modern and efficient engines. On takeoff it wasn't just loud; it emitted a bone-jarring, gut-rumbling feeling that bordered on physical pain. You didn't just hear the ripping roar; you felt it.

The airplane had a hush kit, which was mostly cosmetic. It consisted of metal baffles, one set on the back of each engine, supposedly to dampen the noise. The kit looked more like a miniature version of the ass-end of a German V-2 rocket. It was most effective as a prop when airport managers would question you about the deafening noise level we would emit on takeoff.

"You got a hush kit?" they'd ask.

"Yup, we gotta hush kit right here." I'd put my hand on the pointed baffles and pat them like the ears on a Doberman pinscher.

"Well, I heard the last takeoff, and it sure doesn't sound like you have one."

"Oh yeah, state of the art right here." I'd smile.

"Funny, kinda looks like the ass end of a V-2 rocket."

And it guzzled gas. Flying from Los Angeles to Seattle was about as far as you could go without refueling, and even then, the little red low-fuel lights would wink at you as you lined up on the runway to land. One of the most essential jobs in the cockpit was to monitor the fuel, which disappeared faster than a cup of water thrown on a Death Valley parking lot.

When I got my first assignment, which was ferrying an airplane from Van Nuys to Hawthorne, I had a rude awakening. The other pilots I would be paired with were all ex-NASA test pilots and famous movie pilots who could fly rings around me, literally. Their bios left me with quite an inferiority complex.

Tom McMurtry was the senior pilot in the group. He was a former naval aviator and NASA test pilot, known for his work on aircraft such as the triple-sonic YF-12C, the U-2 and F-104, the KC-135 winglets study, and the F-8 Supercritical Wing project, for which he received NASA's Exceptional Service Medal. He also used to fly the B747 that transported the space shuttle between launches—the shuttle carrier aircraft. Quiet and humble, he knew all there was to know about the Learjet, like every airplane he ever flew. I wasn't worthy of getting him a cup of coffee.

Then there was Ace Beall, another former NASA pilot. He also flew the shuttle carrier aircraft, among many others, and was one of the nicest guys I've ever flown with. He would patiently answer my idiotic questions and tolerate my excursions of airspeed and altitude with polite suggestions that I get my act together.

The first 30 minutes we flew together, we had an engine fire warning on climb out and had to return quickly to the Van Nuys airport for an emergency landing. I was grateful for his experience level, especially since I was such a novice in the Learjet.

The other two pilots were Kevin LaRosa and his son, Kevin Jr. Both guys are famous movie pilots and have worked on many feature films. Kevin Sr. has been in the business since about 1984. He's worked on movies ranging from *Miami Vice, Mission Impossible III*, and *Transformers* to older films going back to *Starman, Universal Soldier,* and *The Fugitive*. Kevin Jr. has worked as an aerial coordinator or pilot on *Cloverfield, Iron Man 1, 2,* and *3, The Avengers, Godzilla, Jack Reacher: Never Go Back, King Kong, Transformers: The Last Knight, Jumanji: Welcome to the Jungle, CSI, NCIS, Ant-Man and the Wasp,* and on and on.

The truth is I had no business flying formation at all. I had been a straight-and-level type of pilot for a long time, had never been in the military, had never flown formation, and flew mostly big airplanes. The closest thing to this gig was learning to do aerobatics in high school and scaring my friend Eddie. This work mostly involved positioning the camera platform aircraft close to another plane in formation flying.

Despite flying airplanes since I was 16 years old, I felt like a total rookie around these guys. They could do things with the plane that defied physics. After a short time, I threw myself on their mercy and explained I had never been trained to formation fly, to which they knowingly said, "Uh huh." When they gave me the chance to try, I couldn't do it if my life depended on it. It was like patting your head with one hand and rubbing your stomach with the other.

I flew the most with Kevin Jr. He knew I couldn't find my ass with both hands when it came to formation flying, but he tutored me and occasionally let me give it a shot. Most of the time, he had me be the target aircraft, which meant I just flew straight and level, like any novice could do, while the subject flew formation on us. It was the same feeling I had on Christmas Eve when I was asked to confine my decorating talents solely to the back of the tree. I was still involved but in a much-diminished role.

We were all a lot safer that way. I'd take off and give control to the other pilot while he joined up with the target aircraft. I'd monitor systems like the rapidly depleting fuel and coordinate with Air Traffic Control. Then I would sit back and watch them do their magic. I was the aviation version of a porn fluffer. I did all the support work, and then watched the other guy have all the fun.

Almost all my missions involved shooting airliners for Boeing customers, as there was a steady stream of aircraft coming out of their factories in the Seattle area. We'd fly up from Hawthorne to Boeing Field or Everett Field, conduct a briefing with the Boeing test pilots who flew the target aircraft, then head out to the western portion of Washington State. The mountains of the Olympic State Park and the Pacific shoreline provided perfect backdrops for the shots.

One of my first missions was to shoot a brand-new Cathay Pacific Cargo B747-8, the biggest Boeing there is. Kevin Jr. and I took off behind the big jet and raced west from Boeing Field to rendezvous with it. As we got closer and closer, my eyes widened. The B747 looks enormous no matter what your perspective. We got as close as I thought possible, then we got closer. In fact, we got so close I could clearly see the faces of the Boeing pilots we met in the preflight briefing. This was unnerving to me because I'd spent my entire career trying to stay far, far away from other airplanes.

As we passed in front of the giant airplane, the air being displaced by the bulbous nose pushed us away like the bow wave of a cruise ship, like a force field that helped keep us separated.

On the way back from these trips we would head low over the mountains so the folks in the back could shoot stock footage of the beautiful cloud formations that surrounded the mountains. Wolfe Air often sold this footage to other customers. Although we always had the peaks in clear sight and a plan to get away from them if something happened, we invariably triggered the low-altitude alerts that are a built-in safety net in Air Traffic Control radar.

"Hey, November 49 Whiskey Alpha, you see that terrain at your twelve o'clock position?" the controller would say.

"Affirmative, we have it in sight, 9 Whiskey Alpha," I'd reply.

A few minutes later: "Ah, are you sure you see it? Getting a low-altitude alert on you. Again." I think the controllers wanted to make sure they would be off the hook if we screwed up and augured into the side of the mountain while capturing stunning footage.

"Yes, we have terrain in sight, 9 Whiskey Alpha."

And it was breathtaking.

Even if you have a rough plan for where you want to go with your career, opportunities will sometimes drop into your lap. For me, it was working for Dan. While you can't always foresee what may come your way, always keep your eye on these windows of opportunity.

CHAPTER 15

RE-CREATING THE MIRACLE ON THE HUDSON

Start where you are. Use what you have. Do what you can.

—Arthur Ashe

There is this classic TV show called *MacGyver*. He's an action hero who can pretty much take a stick of gum and repair a cracked engine cowling with it. He's a man who is incredibly resourceful with whatever is at his disposal. While you may think you couldn't be that clever, if push came to shove, you might surprise yourself. One of the best examples of real-life resourcefulness and heroism happened on a brisk and brilliant winter day on January 15, 2009.

US Airways Flight 1549 had taken off from LaGuardia Airport bound for Charlotte when, at 2,800 feet, it encountered a flock of Canadian geese. Both engines failed, and in a desperate and skillful effort, Captain Chesley "Sully" Sullenberger, assisted by First Officer Jeff Skiles, performed a textbook water landing of the crippled aircraft in the only open area in their path: the Hudson River. Everyone survived.

It was called "the miracle on the Hudson" because it really was. Nothing exactly like that had ever happened before. It was not just any flight but one of the most miraculous and talked-about water landings ever. Sully and his first officer used every minute of training, every hour of experience, and all their resourcefulness to take a hopeless situation and turn it into aviation history.

Six years later, when I was working for Virgin America, I received a call from our VP of Branding and Communications, Abby Lunardini. Clint Eastwood had signed on to direct a feature film about Sully's life. Sully would be played by Tom Hanks, and Skiles would be played by Aaron Eckhart. Would I be willing to make our flight simulator available to give the actors some instruction on how to look like authentic airline pilots?

I called Virgin's Director of Flight Training, Chris Owens, to figure out a game plan. Chris and I contacted Sully via email and asked the basic question: What are you trying to accomplish?

Sully said his main goal was to provide the actors with information that would help them play their roles convincingly. He wanted to demonstrate the event to them, from brake release to 2,800 feet through the landing on the Hudson, then get each of them comfortable in their respective seats, following the standard operating procedures and reading checklists. Ultimately, he wanted Tom in the left seat and Aaron in the right and to allow them to perform their duties in real time.

Sully planned to show up at 10:00 a.m., two hours before the rest of our guests. Chris would operate the simulator, and Sully and I would fly the water landing profile a few times in the simulator. Clint Eastwood would drive up from his home in Carmel, and Tom Hanks, Aaron Eckhart, videographer Liz Radley, and producer Tim Moore would fly up from LA to meet at the training facility at noon.

We sketched out an outline for the actors, with about an hour of briefing followed by some simulator practice. There was plenty of information available about the flight, and we had a copy of the NTSB final report and cockpit voice recorder transcript.

A few days before Sully showed up, I called a friend who was a former long-time US Airways captain and asked him if he knew Sully.

"I'm the only guy from US Airways who will admit that I don't know Sully!"

Apparently, after the historic event, almost every pilot at the airline claimed they were best buddies with him.

Sully was right on time. He took the receptionist aback. She immediately recognized him and showed him in. We chatted for a bit about the industry, my time at United, and the start of his career at Pacific Southwest Airlines. We then traded names to see if we had any people in common in the industry. I found him to be articulate, professional, and humble. I told him this event must have changed his life.

"Immediately, utterly, and forever," he said.

As we settled into the simulator, I asked Sully if he'd re-created the event since the incident. He'd had plenty of opportunities during his regular recurrent training in the US Airways simulator.

"No, I did it once for real and didn't want to do it again," he said.

It wasn't until later that I thought I understood. I would imagine what would happen if, for whatever reason, I didn't perform flawlessly in the simulator after the actual event. People would say it was pure luck, diminishing that remarkable accomplishment. Now, more than six years after the event, with a small group of us in the simulator, I would have felt more comfortable trying it.

So today was the day.

We started with the simulator positioned at LaGuardia gate 21, the same one that Flight 1549 used that day. Sully was a bit somber, very professional, and totally focused on the task, as I'm sure he was on that day. He wanted to use the US Airways procedures and checklists, which he brought along, and I did my best to familiarize myself with them. Although lots of airlines fly the A320, most tailor their procedures to their specific operations.

Using the transcript from the doomed aircraft's voice recorder, we attempted to duplicate everything that happened and was said that day, trying to get the words exactly right. We pushed back, started engines, and taxied to runway 04 at LaGuardia, using the precise routing of the actual flight. Since it was First Officer Skiles's turn to fly, I would make the takeoff from the right seat. We completed the before-takeoff checklist, and I advanced the power.

Sully made the standard callouts: "80." We cross-checked the airspeed indicators.

"Checked," I replied.

"V1, rotate. Positive rate."

"Gear up, please," I said in the exact polite manner used by Skiles.

Sully moved the wheel-shaped lever to raise the landing gear. Chris simulated the air traffic controller. "Cactus 1549, contact New York departure, good day." Cactus was the US Airways radio call sign.

Sully replied, "Good day," and changed the radio frequency from the LaGuardia tower to the radar departure controller. "Cactus 1549, 700, climbing 5,000," he said.

As Sully retracted the flaps, he said, quite ironically, "What a view of the Hudson today."

"Flaps up, after-takeoff checklist," said Skiles.

"After-takeoff checklist complete," Sully said. Three seconds later, he said, "Birds."

Chris had inserted birds into the simulator visual at 2,800 feet, which flickered by with a computer-generated thump. He next simulated the dual engine failure—first, the right engine rolled back to idle, then the left engine. It was difficult for Chris to manage this because there is no one button to simulate this rare failure. He had to select "flameout" then "severe damage" on each engine to replicate the event.

As the engine power decreased, Sully selected the engine ignition to "on" and started the auxiliary power unit (APU), a small jet engine in the tail that provides electricity and pneumatic air, which can help start an engine. Neither of these steps was done with reference to a procedure. They were just what an experienced pilot would do under these circumstances. As it turned out, starting the APU assured that the aircraft would be electrically powered throughout the water landing, as the engine-driven generators were compromised. That step was a long way down the emergency checklist, and I'm not sure they would have gotten that far by the time they hit the water.

Two seconds later, Sully said, "My aircraft," and took control of the jet.

We ran the checklist and stayed true to the actual events as much as possible. The emergency checklist was very long, and with all the distractions, it's a wonder that Skiles got as far down the list as he did.

Like on January 15, 2009, we made a left descending turn and skimmed over the George Washington Bridge, and Sully again made a successful water landing in the Hudson. However, instead of the aircraft yawing to face Manhattan, for some reason we veered right to face the New Jersey side, which Sully immediately noticed.

"That's not accurate," he said. "After we stopped moving, I remember the eerie feeling of staring out at the Manhattan skyline."

We figured the wind direction was not set correctly in the simulation. Chris corrected the wind, and we tried it again.

We ran the scenario two more times, getting closer to the actual voice recorder transcript with each one. Every time, Sully landed successfully.

The phone in the flight simulator rang. Chris answered it.

"They're here," he said, referring to Hanks, Eckhart, Eastwood, and the rest of the crew.

That morning I had the privilege of recreating this historic event with Sully. Now it was time for us to teach Tom Hanks how to do it.

Sully and I got out of the simulator and headed to the break room. Inside, people were mingling.

"Hi. I'm Tom."

That's how Tom Hanks introduced himself, smiling and extending his hand. Although he had grown a beard, apparently for the movie *The Circle,* I'm pretty sure he knew that I knew his last name. He was dressed casually in a black shirt with the tail out and jeans.

They all greeted Sully in a way that made me think they had met before.

Aaron Eckhart introduced himself. He was wearing a white T-shirt and jeans and sported a goatee.

Clint showed up a few minutes later, wearing chinos and a polo shirt. Both Tom and Aaron said, "Hi, boss!" illustrating that no matter how famous you are, everyone has a boss.

The first thing we did was take lunch orders.

"Tom?"

"Turkey."

"Aaron?"

"Turkey."

"Tim?

"Turkey."

Turkey, the meal of the movie people.

We took seats around the conference table, and Chris handed out our rough outline for the day.

Sully talked about the demeanor of an airline pilot. Quietly confident but not arrogant. A pilot's movements on the flight deck are deliberate, not rushed. A good pilot knows where to reach for the switch that he's touched a thousand times, without looking. Physical flying is a series of small corrections on the side stick controller—there aren't many big movements if you are doing it correctly. A good pilot does not appear to be doing very much.

Tom and Aaron had their actor's notebooks out and were scribbling notes furiously. I was amazed at their attention to every detail. After all, they weren't actually going to fly the plane—this was just pretend.

Tom said their goal was to be as realistic as possible. "I did a prison movie that took place in 1935." (*The Green Mile*, based on the Stephen King novel.) "We had total poetic license there. Prison guards in Louisiana didn't wear uniforms, and they certainly didn't carry guns, but we did both in the movie."

He took a bite of his turkey sandwich and continued. "There are so many bad airline movies out there, starting with the original *Airport*, where Dean Martin was the captain. So the bar isn't set very high."

He added that they wanted to be authentic. "But it is a movie, so I can't guarantee there won't be some sparks shooting out from somewhere!"

I asked Sully if he'd seen the NBC series *30 Rock*, which had a storyline about an airline pilot where he was mentioned.

Tom jumped in. "Yeah, I remember that. Matt Damon played an airline pilot. When Liz Lemon first meets him in a lobby, he's in his pilot uniform, and she says, 'Are you a doorman?' and he says, 'Yeah, I'm a doorman—to the sky!'"

I said there was another funny episode where the Jack Donaghy character, played by Alec Baldwin, meets the pilot and wants to pick his brain about a talk show idea starring Sully.

The Matt Damon character responds: "I've met Sully. He isn't so great. You know what a great pilot would have done? Not hit the birds. That's what I do every day, not hit birds. Where's my ticket to the Grammys?"

Sully shook his head and grinned. I wondered how comfortable he was with being a part of pop culture.

We went on to discuss his state of mind during the incident. "The only other time I had this feeling of being disconnected was when I had a serious mountain biking accident. Everything seemed to happen in slow motion."

Tom said, "I hope there wasn't a bird involved."

Sully smiled. "No birds."

After getting acquainted and setting out the basics, it was time to get into the technical details. We positioned the two actors in our "paper trainer" in the corner of the room, a replica of the cockpit with detailed pictures of the overhead, forward, and pedestal panels.

Chris worked with them on their standard operating procedures, or SOPs, the series of steps that define what a pilot does from the time they arrive at the airplane until they leave the flight deck at the end the trip. Both Tom and Aaron continued to jot copious notes into their well-worn notebooks.

An expert on the A320, Chris was very enthusiastic about its many capabilities. At one point Aaron asked a technical question about the flight control system. Chris got a bit excited and started talking about the technical intricacies of the airplane. He also talked about Normal Fight Control Law, Alternate Law, and Direct Law, and how the aircraft reverts to each one.

"The Airbus is more complicated than some other airliners, and the systems also interact with each other in ways that can be confusing," Chris said. That might be helpful to a real airline pilot, but these guys were actors.

As thorough as the actors were, there was a limit. Tom and Aaron quickly glazed over, and Tom leaned back in his chair and looked at the ceiling. Then, he leaned forward and said politely, "Chris, we have to look like we know what we are doing for only three and a half minutes."

Chris paused and laughed, and we continued with the briefing.

Then it was time to get into the flight simulator.

Sully took the captain's seat on the left, and I took the first officer's seat on the right with Clint's videographer, Liz Radley, recording everything on a handheld camera. Sully and I re-created the flight from pushback to the splashdown, in real time. We then repositioned to the gate and did it again, this time slowly enough so that Tom and Aaron could capture every step.

Next, it was their turn to fly. Tom got in the left seat, and I remained in the right. I walked him through the entire profile, but this time, like the Matt Damon character, we didn't hit the birds. I had him fly straight out and let him get a feel for the flight controls.

Tom was self-deprecating, but having done a lot of these demonstrations, I have to say he got the hang of it very quickly, making an entirely acceptable landing.

We switched seats and went through the same routine with Aaron, who also made a decent landing.

Clint was very quiet in the simulator, and at the time, I wasn't sure what he was doing other than watching. Later, he would say during an interview that he spent that day visualizing how he would shoot and cut these dramatic scenes together. Like we told Tom and Aaron, when a pilot is doing a good job flying, it doesn't look like he is doing very much. I suppose that's also true for an acclaimed movie director.

From the back of the simulator, Clint, a pilot himself, finally spoke up and said, "Those landings were awful."

I turned around in my seat. "Clint, would you like to give it a try?"

In his most authentic Dirty Harry voice, Clint declined. "A man's got to know his limitations."

We took a break, and I had a moment alone with Tom outside of the simulator bay.

"You know, not just anyone would be able to do this. Successfully ditching an airliner is unheard of," I said.

Tom said, "Yeah, after getting to know Sully, I figured that out."

We finished up, shot a few photos for posterity, and they were off.

We spent only that one day with the actors, but I hoped it gave them a solid introduction to the world of airline pilots. Fortunately, Sully spent much more time with them during shooting, and his input was critical to making the movie authentic.

Months later, on September 8, 2016, I was invited to the cast and crew premiere of *Sully* at the Steven Ross Theater at Warner Bros. studios in Burbank. The event was more crew than cast. If there were actors there, I didn't recognize them, but it was fun nonetheless. The lead actors had attended a VIP showing in New York the previous day.

I talked to Tim Moore, the producer we worked with at the simulator, who said Sully and Clint were pleased with the results.

Before the premiere, the producers introduced the movie from the front of the theater. They said the film got great reviews from the *Wall Street Journal, New York Times, Washington Post*, and *Los Angeles Times*.

I also talked to Liz Radley, who said the video they shot with us in the Virgin America simulator was invaluable. She and the actors relied on the footage they shot with us to get the visuals right. "You guys really nailed it," Liz said. "The profile was perfect, and so were the sight lines. I actually wanted to fly back to your simulator to do more, but we were already shooting on the east coast."

She added that the actors studied the video and the simulator instruction before shooting the cockpit scenes.

Tim said, "The boss [Clint] liked it, and Sully liked it. That's what matters. Clint is very proud of the film."

As you might expect, the crowd was fairly riveted to the movie. From a technical standpoint, it was very accurate. I think any airline pilot would say the flying portions were authentic. The actors took great pains to get even the smallest detail right. All that note-taking apparently paid off. They took an incident that lasted 208 seconds and did a great job turning it into a gripping 90 minutes.

I can't tell you what I would have done in Sully's shoes. No one else has ever been in that position. But in a moment when lives depended on it, he used every available resource—including his training, experience, intuition, faith, and luck—to land safely on the Hudson.

The next time you believe you lack all the tools you need to do your job, think of MacGyver or Sully. I'm sure you'll find a stick of chewing gum or divine inspiration somewhere.

CHAPTER 16

R-E-S-P-E-C-T—
GIVE SKILL ITS PROPS

We are what we repeatedly do. Excellence, then, is not an act,
but a habit.

—Will Durant

Would you ever hire the plumber with the worst reviews on Yelp to fix your toilet? Probably not.

We all aspire to the best of everything—to have it, to be it. So when you come across people whose approach to their career is in every way excellent, you can't help but stand back and admire them. They didn't just fall out of bed exceptional. It took dedication, work, grit, and practice, practice, practice. Like my friend Kevin Newman, an airline pilot who flew F-16s in the Air National Guard at Buckley Air Force Base just east of Denver, Colorado.

"Do you want to fly an F-16 fighter jet?"

It was a ridiculous question for somebody who loves airplanes. Who would turn that down? "You can arrange that?" I asked him.

"You bet."

This notion was a little problematic for two reasons. First, the F-16 typically has only one seat. However, his unit had recently and temporarily come into possession of a two-seat F-16 that was used mainly as a trainer and for familiarization rides for taxpayers like me.

Second, I really didn't know Kevin that well, and I was going to put my life in his hands in a supersonic, highly sophisticated war machine.

The F-16 is officially called the Fighting Falcon, but pilots thought that sounded like a pansy-ass name, so they always referred to it with a much more menacing name, Viper. It is a single-engine supersonic fighter aircraft originally developed by General Dynamics (now Lockheed Martin) for the US Air Force. It was designed as a multirole fighter, which means it shoots down enemy aircraft and carries out light attack. It later evolved into a successful all-weather aircraft. Thousands of them were produced and are deployed around the world, in service to the United States and our allies.

I wanted to think this whole operation was on the level, but there were indications that it was not. I overheard someone mention that the commanding officer of the unit was not in town on the days I was there, so I'm not sure this boondoggle was ever officially approved. Nevertheless, due to my fascination with high-performance airplanes, I suppressed my doubts and RSVP'd in the affirmative.

I was directed to show up at the Air National Guard the day before the flight for my orientation, then meet Kevin in the Officers' Club for a drink.

I was met by a serious looking National Guard–enlisted man named Bart, my instructor. He took me into an equipment room and fitted me for a flight suit, a G-suit and helmet, then went through a very long and scripted briefing on how to wear the equipment. Tubes inside the G-suit automatically inflate as the G-forces increase, squeezing your legs to prevent the blood from pooling there, keeping it near your brain and other vital organs where you need it when flying a fighter jet.

Later, I would find out that Bart had issued me only half a G-suit because the real pilots wear the pants *and* a shirt. I assumed this was because we weren't actually going into combat, but like many things that day, I trusted that he knew what he was doing.

Bart then informed me that we would now do egress training, which is required for anyone who goes up in a fighter jet. Egress is a nice way of saying they would teach me how to eject from the aircraft.

"Okay, whoa, now. Eject? How often does that happen?" I asked.

"Not very often, but you have to be ready for anything," Bart replied.

I checked, and "not very often" means there have been over 600 live ejections using this model of ejection seat, called the ACES II. I'm not sure what that rate would be, but it seemed more common than "not very often."

The idea here is that in a dire emergency, the ejection seat will propel the pilot up and away from the aircraft, the parachute will open, and the pilot will drift gently to the ground. That's the theory, anyway.

The ejection seat consists of a rocket motor that is triggered by pulling a yellow handle between the pilot's knees. The seat is smart and adjusts the thrust based on your aircraft speed, altitude, and other factors. It'll even eject you if you are on the ground, standing still.

"It's the thrust you can trust," Bart said reassuringly.

Obviously, the ejection seat must be sequenced so that the canopy pops off first, and then the rocket fires. Otherwise, the pilot could be propelled forcefully and tragically into the unyielding canopy, just like the character Goose in the movie *Top Gun*, with the same result. Bart told me this "probably" can't happen due to safeguards in the seat.

Probably?

A friend of mine, Lew Kosich, actually survived being ejected from a fighter jet while still on the ground. He was in an F-14 Tomcat on the USS *John F. Kennedy*, which happens to be the same type of airplane that Tom Cruise pretended to fly in *Top Gun*. The F-14 is like the F-16 except it has two engines and two crew members: a pilot in front and a radar intercept officer (RIO) in the back. Lew and his back-seater were part of NATO exercises about 60 miles north of Scotland in the North Sea. At the time, it was the largest gathering of Allied ships since D-Day, so there were a lot of witnesses.

The seas were rough. It was cold, and the winds were fierce. The deck was crowded with other warplanes that were fueled, armed, and waiting to launch. Lew was waiting to be hooked up to the catapult that would launch him into the air when a sudden malfunction in the computer controlling the throttle applied full power to both engines. His airplane was headed directly for a line of aircraft waiting on the wet and slippery deck.

In a split second, Lew steered the jet away from the other planes to an empty spot on the edge of the deck. He and his back-seater ejected as the F-14 clumsily nosed over the end of the deck, well below flying speed, and crashed into the ocean. Lucky for them, the wind blew their chutes right back over the deck, and they miraculously landed on the ship near where his airplane used to be, sparing them an icy dunk in the North Sea. But with all that wind, they were moving at a healthy clip when they landed. The radar officer broke his knee, and Lew injured his hip, which bothers him to this day. So much for drifting gently to the ground.

This was yet another reason why I was nervous about this whole thing and was putting a heck of a lot of faith in Kevin—and the equipment. As Lew will tell you, ejecting is something you do as an absolute last resort—and something I never wanted to do at all.

My instructor had me climb into a training device that resembled a stripped-down, wooden F-16 cockpit. It looked like some high school kid built it in wood shop, but I'm sure the manufacturer charged the military a pretty penny for it.

I still remember three specific things he taught me about ejecting.

One: pull on the big yellow handle between your legs.

Two: make darn sure your shoulder and crotch straps, which attach your body to the ejection seat and parachute, are very, very tight.

And three: if you see the other guy eject, you'd better eject, too.

Once we completed our training, I rendezvoused with Kevin in the Officers' Club for a drink. He said it was a tradition to drink Jack Daniel's and Coke the day before a mission. Kevin had flown in combat in the Middle East, so I figured he knew what he was talking about.

Unfortunately, I hate Jack Daniel's. The odor, the color, even the bottle all turn me off, and for good reason. There was a substantial supply of it in the Robbins' basement, the one that was decorated like a Western saloon—the place we went as teenagers for illicit alcohol.

Of course, Kevin knew none of this, but it was why I can barely stomach whiskey, even today.

Nonetheless, I didn't want to offend Kevin since the next day my life would depend on him. I sidled up to the bar. We were the only ones in the room. He pulled out his personal bottle of Jack, mixed it with Coke he got from somewhere, and we toasted. I tried to exhale through my nose while sipping so I wouldn't smell it, trying to stifle my gag reflex.

"So what do you want to do tomorrow? Pull Gs, go low and fast?" Kevin asked.

"If I were younger, I'd want to pull Gs," I said. "But at my age, I'd rather just fly low and fast."

Pulling Gs is painful. I recalled the day I scared Eddie. We momentarily pulled just four Gs. That was horrible, and I was a young and fit 17-year-old at the time. The F-16 can pull up to 9 Gs. In fact, the controls are programmed to prevent pulling more than nine Gs, which could overstress the airplane—and you. Even with a G-suit, or half of one, most people start blacking out well before nine Gs. It all depends on your physiological makeup, conditioning, and experience. Since I was deficient in all three, I opted for low and fast instead of high Gs.

Kevin explained the sequence of events that occurs before you lose consciousness.

"First, at about four Gs for 15-30 seconds, your color vision goes to black and white, but you still have your peripheral vision." That was encouraging.

"Next you lose peripheral vision, and then you get tunnel vision, where you can see only straight ahead. With a few more Gs, that tunnel you are staring at fades slowly to black, and you are close to unconsciousness. That's a good time to ease up on the controls," Kevin said.

"I'm not planning to go that far," I said.

"You can counteract it by performing the anti-G-straining maneuver," Kevin added.

"The what?"

"You breathe rapidly while flexing your muscles in the legs and abdomen," Kevin said.

I looked at him with a bewildered expression.

"Let me put it another way: you breathe hard while bearing down like you are having a bowel movement." That I could understand. I was just hoping that during this exercise, I would not actually have one.

"All good? We'll avoid a lot of Gs and just head south toward Colorado Springs. Maybe fly through some of the mountain passes," Kevin said.

We would be heading south over the mountains between Denver and Colorado Springs, to Alert Area 260, where "unusual" aeronautical activity is conducted. That was going to be us.

Out of politeness, I finished my drink, set down the glass, and started to stand up. Kevin, who was already a drink ahead of me, immediately refilled it.

"You don't have to be anywhere, do you?" Kevin said.

"Uh, no, not really." I hunkered down for another one.

The next morning I showed up early to retrieve my equipment. I dressed in the ready room, which looked more like a locker room, and walked out to the flight line to meet Kevin. He exhibited no ill effects from the Jack Daniel's. As directed, I had my harness very, very tight. My flight suit was puffing out from beneath the crotch straps that were painfully compressing my most sensitive male parts.

Kevin shook my hand, and his eyes lowered to inspect my attire. "Aww, jeez," he said sympathetically. "You gotta loosen up that crotch strap, man."

"No, Bart told me it has to be very tight in case we have to eject."

"We. Are. Not. Going. To. Eject. Today," Kevin said, enunciating every word for effect.

We walked out to where our jet awaited us, along with a crew chief who would help us start the engine and guide us away.

The F-16 was a very cool-looking airplane. Its needle nose, with the gaping mouth-like engine inlet below, gave it an evil appearance. The raked tail made it look like it was moving while standing still, even more than the Learjet. No wonder the pilots nicknamed it Viper.

But the main feature that caught my eye was the enormous engine. Compared to other aircraft, the Viper looked like it was almost *all* engine, with a couple of tiny wings bolted onto it plus a very small tail that was dominated by the engine outlet. The tail of the engine is where the afterburner is located, where raw fuel is dumped and ignited to provide maximum power for short durations. It is like a giant, white-hot blast furnace that propels the plane through the sky.

With the afterburner going at maximum power, the Viper can fly at a little more than twice the speed of sound. Put another way, Mach 2 is about 2,200 feet per second, and a .45 caliber bullet travels at about 830 feet per second. When you fly the F-16, you really are like Superman, faster than a speeding bullet.

At that incredible speed, the airplane burns about 60,000 pounds of fuel per hour, but it holds only 8,000 pounds of fuel internally, so it can't do it for very long. That's probably why there were two huge fuel tanks hanging from the bottom of the wings, giving the jet a muscular look.

We climbed up a metal ladder, and Kevin helped me strap into the back seat. The cockpit had a big bubble canopy that provided excellent visibility, a side stick control that used electronic signals, called fly by wire, to control it, and a serious-looking throttle handle that modulated the massive engine. You don't actually fly the F-16; you give control inputs through the stick that is connected to computers. They, in turn, manipulate the control surfaces.

Later, I found out that the F-16 has another nickname: Lawn Dart. Apparently, the early fly-by-wire system wasn't without a few serious bugs. Occasionally, the flight control computers would malfunction. The airplane would pitch nose down uncontrollably, and that pointy nose and everything behind it would end up buried deep in the ground, like a lawn dart.

Once settled in, I put on my helmet and attached my oxygen mask. I was a little claustrophobic, but once my breathing returned to normal after the exertion of climbing in, I felt okay.

Kevin climbed into the front seat, got strapped in, and closed the canopy. He signaled to the crew chief, and the big engine rumbled to life. "Can you hear me okay?" Kevin said through the interphone.

"Loud and clear," I replied.

As we taxied out, Kevin told me what to expect. "We will take off, level off a couple of feet over the runway to gain some speed. Then I'll pull straight up to the vertical, and we'll climb to 15,000 feet and level off. After that, it's all yours."

All mine? I thought with a jolt of trepidation.

Once the big chunk of airspace above us was cleared of anything we could collide with, we were cleared for takeoff.

Kevin lined up on the runway, added full power, and we accelerated like the Rock 'N' Roller Coaster ride at Disney's Hollywood Studios. We were soon airborne. Kevin raised the landing gear, and he leveled off at what felt like inches over the runway. Our speed grew quickly to about 350 knots, and suddenly he pulled the nose to vertical. We were on our backs, climbing straight up.

"Look over your shoulder!" Kevin said.

I looked back and saw something I'd never seen before in an airplane. The runway seemed like it was right under us—because it pretty much was.

We were quickly approaching 15,000 feet, and Kevin continued to pull the nose back until we were upside down. Then he abruptly rolled us level.

"You have control," he said with a chuckle.

I gently grabbed the stick. The slightest pressure made the airplane's attitude change, and at first, I grossly over controlled.

"Just play around with it a little," Kevin said. Slowly, I got more comfortable with the stick.

"Try a turn to the right," Kevin said. As in every other airplane I'd flown, I applied right stick. The jet banked about 30 degrees but didn't turn.

"You have to pull back to make a turn. Otherwise, it will just fly straight ahead with the wings banked." Like I said, all engine.

I tried again, rolling right, and when I pulled back, the heading began to change.

"That's different," I said.

"That's what you have to do in this plane," he said. "Try a roll."

I applied a small amount of right stick. Before I knew it, we had rolled all the way around and past the level point at an incredibly fast roll rate. "Wow, that's sensitive," I said as I got us back to wings level.

Heading south, I experimented with the controls, turning left then right as we worked our way to the military operating area near Colorado Springs. The controller soon released us to fly on our own.

"Let's take it down low."

We descended quickly until we were well below the mountain peaks that surrounded us. As we dropped, our airspeed increased to 400 knots. I'd never seen an airspeed indicator with such a high value, which topped out at 800 knots.

"Follow this mountain pass ahead of us."

I could only imagine what this looked like from the ground. It was like the *Star Wars* scene where they attacked the Death Star. My only limitation was to make sure we didn't exceed the speed of sound, which would trigger a sonic boom and many angry phone calls to the National Guard. Or run into the mountain.

Flying the jet was like straddling an engine. It was all about power. I thought about the movie *Dr. Strangelove* where actor Slim Pickens, atop a nuclear bomb in the belly of a B-52, is accidentally released, and he gleefully rides the bomb all the way to the ground as it detonates. That engine underneath me felt like a nuke. That's about how in control I felt when flying the F-16.

We buzzed around down low for a while, and then headed back toward the airport.

Everything was going great until Kevin said, "Do you want to join the nine G club?"

"You mean, pull nine Gs?" I asked.

"Yeah, just roll into a bank, then pull back on the stick really hard."

"No, that's okay. How about I join the seven G club instead?" I figured that would beat my record with Eddie by at least three Gs.

"Your call," Kevin said.

I rolled into a bank and hauled back on the stick. As the Gs built, my half G-suit began to inflate, squeezing my legs so that the blood in my head would stay there. As I pulled back on the stick, I was pushed harder and harder into my seat. It was getting hard to breathe, as if a sumo wrestler were planted on my stomach. Even at the seven G level, my field of vision began to narrow, just like I was warned. Performing the anti-G straining maneuver never crossed my mind.

That was enough. I let up on the stick, and we returned to normal flight. The sumo wrestler disappeared, and my vision returned, but I was done.

I rarely get motion sickness, but the combination of the low-level flight, the G-forces, and the residue of the Jack Daniel's in my liver took their toll. I was glad we were heading back to the airport.

"How about we do a few takeoffs and landings?" Kevin said.

"Sure," I said half-heartedly. "Sounds great."

We were soon back on approach to Buckley. Kevin made a good landing, then gunned the engine and took off for another.

"You know, maybe we should just land now," I said, breathing deeply. I could identify precisely how Eddie must have felt after my poorly executed split S.

"Okay, sure. This one will be a full stop."

Thank you, Kevin, I said to myself.

We circled around and were soon back on the ground. As we cleared the runway, I removed my oxygen mask and pointed the one small round air vent in front of me directly at my face. If I could've reached it, I would have put my mouth over the vent to suck in as much fresh air as possible.

We parked, the crewman put the metal stairs against the side of the plane, and I shakily climbed down.

I didn't kiss the ground, but I would have if no one had been looking. After experiencing a hair-raising high-speed, low-level buzz job, a breathtaking seven G turn, and a visit from a sumo wrestler, I realized I couldn't have been in more capable hands than those of my friend Kevin.

I had a newfound respect for the skill F-16 pilots like Kevin master over countless flight hours in grueling conditions, never happy with "just good enough."

CHAPTER 17

BOLDLY BEING VIRGIN

> We can't solve problems by using the same kind of thinking
> we used when we created them.
>
> —Albert Einstein

We advance, improve, learn, and make the world a better place because of people who refuse to do things the way they have always been done. When you think business innovator, Richard Branson immediately comes to mind.

I was working at Virgin America for only two weeks when I met him. He was in Los Angeles supporting the launch of our first flight to Las Vegas.

Though there was a multitude of companies under the Virgin brand, Branson had a particular soft spot for Virgin America, the crown jewel of his holdings in the United States. When we started flying a new city pair, he invariably showed up. Without Branson, we'd get about five reporters. With Branson, we'd get 50. His mere presence guaranteed some very valuable free publicity.

Branson walked in the Virgin America Club at Los Angeles International Airport and was immediately flanked by three leggy chorus girls, complete with red-and-silver outfits with tall feathered hats, whom we hired to support the launch. He posed for photos with them, then met and posed with just about everyone in the club. He has an easygoing manner and seemed to connect with almost anyone.

When he met me, he shook my hand and seemed genuinely happy to see me. Branson rode with us and a planeload of VIPs on the short flight from Los Angeles to Las Vegas. Once we were airborne, he walked the aisle of the airplane, talking to everyone.

During that flight we launched a "get lucky" text chat system onboard the airplane, where passengers could send a drink or cocktail to another seat. It was a fun little product tweak that received national and global press exposure, basically for free. It was called "How Richard Does Vegas."

When we arrived, the gate area was packed with press as Branson donned a pilot hat and black sequined pilot jacket. He gave a quick talk about how vital the Las Vegas market was for Virgin and hosted a cocktail reception in an area near the gate.

Branson is one of the most successful entrepreneurs in history. One book he wrote is called *Screw It, Let's Do It*. While that is not the philosophy we embraced when operating the airplanes, it is a smart way to look at marketing. He is also well known for thinking outside the box and pulling crazy stunts that help draw attention to his brand. He's not afraid to use novel strategies to achieve his goals.

In 2013, he made a bet with Tony Fernandes, AirAsia's CEO, over whose F1 racing team would finish higher at the 2010 Formula 1 Grand Prix: Branson's Virgin Racing or Fernandes's Team Lotus. Whoever lost would have to serve as a flight attendant on the other's airline.

Branson lost. So in 2011, he had to put on a woman's sexy red AirAsia flight attendant uniform for a 13-hour London to

Kuala Lumpur flight. He also shaved his legs, since Fernandes's airline doesn't allow "hairy stewardesses" (though he was allowed to keep his beard). He had to serve meals and drinks to Tony Fernandes and 250 other passengers. This was not the first time Branson dressed as a woman—he wore a white wedding dress for the launch of Virgin Brides in 1996.

Virgin America's marketing department had a relatively small budget. The airline relied on a strong social media presence—and Branson—to make the airline seem more substantial than it was.

One way to accomplish this was to come up with an annual April Fool's prank. The last one before the airline was taken over by Alaska Air, which put an end to the practice, involved a spoof about changing the company logo.

The concept was a takeoff on Airbnb, the service that lets property owners rent out their homes to travelers. Airbnb rebranded with a controversial new logo in 2014. Pundits variously said it looked like a paper clip, someone's rear end, genitalia, or a heart. Airbnb even named the logo Belo, short for belonging. There was so much confusion that it later had to explain the logo represented people, places, love, and the letter A for Airbnb. I didn't see it.

Virgin produced a bogus video satirizing the self-importance of Silicon Valley as evidenced by the Airbnb fiasco. It starred fictional hipster and creative genius Connor Barnaby, who waxed philosophically about the challenge of creating a new Virgin logo. He was the stereotypical hipster: young, affluent, with a closely cropped beard, small black glasses, multiple beaded wristbands, and a red flannel shirt buttoned to the top. He was frequently seen wearing a scarf. Unseen but strongly inferred was his unwarranted sense of being a snowflake, unique in the world—another hipster characteristic.

"With traveler support"—he held up one hand—"and tech-infused technology"—he held up the other, like holding imaginary breasts—"when you bring these elements together, you begin to understand what is the essence of Virgin," said Barnaby.

"We need to go back to our roots, and go deep," said Luanne Calvert solemnly and sarcastically. Calvert was the head of marketing for Virgin America.

The video later cut to Branson, who explained how he felt the brand "right here" and pointed to his chest. Then we see some of Branson's concept sketches of the things that are important to him: some juvenile tongue-in-cheek doodles with strong sexual innuendo.

"This will be Earth-world changing," said Luanne with mock reverence.

Finally, the logo was revealed, and to me it looked a whole lot like a stylized bikini top.

People who fly on Virgin are used to these pranks and don't take them seriously. Virgin once did a mock promotion with Nest thermostats, claiming that everyone on the plane would be able to adjust the temperature at their seat. Another year, Branson announced that Virgin would move its headquarters to Branson, Missouri, a town of only 10,000 residents. They were close to doing a prank about self-flying airplanes, but I didn't think our pilots would find that very funny, so we dropped it.

We had hoped that our vendors would understand that these were just jokes. During a technical presentation to Virgin America by Safran, a French company that manufactures components for Airbus aircraft, Safran copied the bogus Virgin America bikini top logo into one of its presentation slides. I guess some Safran minion googled "Virgin America logo" and copied the first one that popped up—the counterfeit.

Branson relishes the role of underdog in almost any context. When Virgin America fought to gain two coveted gates at Dallas Love Field, Branson was there in his typical, unconventional way.

Virgin launched a massive social media campaign in the backyard of Southwest Airlines, which controlled all the gates at Love Field except the two that were up for grabs. It was called "Free Love Field" and garnered 27,000 signatures. We planned a big media event, branding Virgin as the little guy and a scrappy start-up that would bring better service and lower fares. We even flew a Virgin America airplane to Love Field for the event. I was the captain, and Mark Bregar, the Virgin America chief pilot, flew as the first officer. I joked with our branding people that we'd be wearing shorts and T-shirts instead of uniforms since this was an empty airplane on a ferry flight, and we wanted to be comfortable.

As we descended into Dallas and lined up with the runway for landing, we noticed several helicopters hovering off to our right.

"I think we are on TV, Steve," said Mark. And he was right. It must have been a slow news day because our landing was indeed being filmed on live TV. We touched down, turned off the runway, and taxied to the north side of the airport. There awaiting us were more reporters with cameras, filming us through the fence.

At about this time Abby was having a stroke. She still thought we were wearing shorts and T-shirts. How would it look if the Virgin pilots stepped off the airplane dressed like two guys who just cleaned out their garage? It would be Bransonesque but not very professional. Fortunately, we were indeed wearing our uniforms, and when Abby saw the live feed, she breathed a huge sigh of relief.

This turned out to be a significant event in Dallas. Virgin sponsored a large party for Dallas VIPs, celebrities, Virgin customers, and anybody who had influence. Branson was the life of the party, at one point standing up next to a fireplace mantel at the VIP pre-party to encourage the crowd to support Virgin's quest for the gates. The main event was held at the House of Blues with country star Kacey Musgraves performing.

Branson released a hilarious video of him composing a love letter to Love Field, which was released the day of the final city council hearing. The scene is softly lit with a romantic saxophone playing in the background. He is seen in his office, fountain pen in hand, drafting the letter.

"My Dearest Love,

From the moment I knew I had a shot at you, you were all that I could think of," he says wistfully.

"Others would keep you all to themselves. I invite competition for your affections. Nay, I demand it. After all, no one should have a monopoly on your love. My virile young planes," he says, stroking the tail of a Virgin America Airbus jet model, "are yearning for your runways. You make my heart soar to the highest heights and my fares drop to the lowest lows. You have the window seat to my heart, kitten."

And then he signs off.

"It's time to let our love take flight, no matter how they try to keep us apart. Your sweetheart, Richie."

All this hype, combined with the public support and near-constant media coverage, did the trick. It all worked, and after a lot of political maneuvering, Virgin was granted those very valuable gates at Love Field.

Branson loves to be creative and cheeky, as evidenced by the names of some of the Virgin airplanes. We had the clever cocktail name "Virgin and Tonic." We had "#nerdbird" in honor of Silicon Valley and our service to San Jose. Our first airplane to fly to Hawaii was named "Pineapple Express," which obviously refers to a strong polar jet stream (although there was a popular movie by the same name). "Legally High" was the name of our first airplane to fly to Denver, which occurred shortly after the state legalized marijuana. I suggested "Air-Canna-Bus," a twist on our aircraft manufacturer Airbus, but it was vetoed.

"You worry about making the planes go, and we'll do the marketing," I was told by Luanne jokingly—I think.

We used to talk about "the curtain" at Virgin America. In front of it was the glitz, music, parties, mood lighting—the brand. Behind it was the serious stuff we did to run a safe operation. We had an outstanding reputation for safety and compliance with the FAA. However, when we told FAA officials we were changing from our animated safety video, which we'd used from day one, to a new one that would be a music video, they were skeptical.

The FAA requires dozens of elements be covered in the video: showing the exits and safety card, demonstrating the use of the life vests and seat belt, etc. In the end you can't use the video until the FAA approves it. It was my job to convince them that this change was a good thing.

The video called for 36 dancers and singers acting out the requirements. This included contortionists, robot dancers, a rapping little kid, and a singing and dancing nun. It featured 14 different dance styles, including B-boy, break dancing, finger-tutting, tango, and waving-just.

Well-known music video and feature film director Jon M. Chu signed on to make the video. The song and lyrics were written by American Idol star Todrick Hall, who is also the main character in the video.

I remember presenting the original script to our FAA principal operations inspector for approval. He left my office to read it and returned a few minutes later. The script was dangling from his hand, pages flayed, and he was distraught.

"I don't know if we can do this," he said. "Did you know you have a dancing nun in here?"

"Yes," I said, "but we'll make sure all the required elements are included."

He looked skeptical, so I opted for a little aversion therapy.

"Check the Air New Zealand website, and watch its safety videos. The company has done some unusual things. Watch the one where the entire crew is wearing nothing but body paint," I said.

"Body paint?"

"Yes. We'll also get you a spreadsheet with all the requirements and check them off so we don't miss any."

Helen Cleary, who coordinated with the FAA, created a very detailed plan for them.

When our inspector took the script back to the FAA office, everyone there seemed to have an opinion. We made 35 changes to the script over the next few weeks to accommodate them. Then it came down to one last item.

In the original script, one of the flight attendants says, "For the .001 percent of you who have never operated a seat belt before, what the (bleep) is wrong with you?" She didn't actually curse, but it was bleeped out on the audio track and represented like this in the required subtitles: "#%&@."

We went around and around but finally gave in. We couldn't delay production any longer. In the final version, she says, "For the .001 percent of you who have never operated a seat belt before—*really?*"

We did win a few disputes, though. The FAA initially told us they didn't like the dancers tossing around the safety information card because it showed disregard for safety. They finally backed down when we explained that highlighting the card might encourage more people to look at it.

During the shoot, which was done on a soundstage in Burbank, we allowed the FAA representatives to attend as technical consultants. I think they were blown away by the glamour of the event, which was pure showbiz.

The video was finally approved, and even the people at FAA headquarters loved it. Anything to get the flying public's attention was good for safety. More importantly, Richard Branson loved it.

The video debuted on a billboard in Times Square on October 29, 2013, and was featured on *The Ellen Show* the same week.

When it was released, it went viral. I was at an event that day at Virgin Produced in Santa Monica to celebrate, and we tallied the hits every few minutes. It got one million views in the first 24 hours. It ultimately racked up 11 million views, and everyone from the *New Yorker*'s theater critic to TechCrunch praised the video.

In 2016, Virgin America was sold to Alaska Air in a deal worth $2.6 billion. In a letter on his blog, Branson wrote, "Our innovative, stylish, guest-focused product and experience (and even our safety video) have made such an impact that our little airline forced the big legacy airlines to step up and find ways to compete. Because I'm not American, the US Department of Transportation stipulated I take some of my shares in Virgin America as nonvoting shares, reducing my influence over any takeover," he wrote. "So there was sadly nothing I could do to stop it."

And so it was done. The Branson era of creative genius, zealous employee commitment, and distinctly different customer service ended.

Branson didn't earn that loyalty from customers and employees just by being clever. True, his bombastic style and over-the-top ideas helped Virgin America shine in comparison to most competitors and created a much bigger wake in an industry choked with fierce competitors. But he always delivered what he promised—and just a bit more. He was a bold innovator in an industry fond of saying, "Because we've always done it that way."

I was fortunate to have worked for Branson. He taught me to keep innovating and deliver on your promises—and then some.

Virgin Airways safety video, https://www.virgin.com/richard-branson/virgin-america.
Branson love letter, https://www.virgin.com/richard-branson/feeling-love.

CHAPTER 18

NUDGE YOUR BUBBLE OF COMFORT

Man cannot discover new oceans unless he has the courage
to lose sight of the shore.

—Andre Gide

Each of us has a different definition of reaching beyond our bubble of comfort. While it's easy to stick to the well-traveled road, you find the most amazing things when you wander off the path. For example, I'd never flown a seaplane, although I had ridden in a few. I didn't need to learn how to fly one, but it was definitely a "bucket list" item. I wanted to see if I could do it.

Bush pilots say that it's the most fun you can have in an airplane. It combines the exhilaration of flight with the delights of boating, along with the additive dangers of both.

There are many places in the United States where you can earn your float rating or, as it says on your pilot certificate, Single Engine Sea rating, even though I accomplished it many miles from the sea in the freshwater lakes of central Florida. However, I admit, Single Engine Sea sounds like a much more impressive accomplishment than Single Engine Fresh Water Lake, so we'll go with that.

One of the more iconic flight schools is Brown's Seaplane Base in Winter Haven, Florida. It has been around since 1963, started by Jack and now run by his son, Jon. They have the basic course down to a science. Day one: show up for ground school, fly, take a break, fly, and go home. Day two: fly again to review everything, then take the FAA oral and flight check. It's like those quickie weekend continuing education courses familiar to doctors and lawyers.

Jack Brown loved seaplanes. He first flew an Aeronca C-3 seaplane on the Kanawha River in West Virginia and flew the Grumman "flying boats" and PBYs during WWII. After that, he became a civilian instructor and test pilot for the US Air Force stationed in central Florida and settled down as the first fixed-base operator at the Winter Haven airport, which is now called Gilbert Field. He later established the seaplane base in 1963 on Lake Jessie.

Like continuing education, these adventures are always more fun to do with another person, especially the part in the evening when you go out for a beer, with plenty of time between bottle and throttle.

I convinced my friend and colleague Al Spain, an accomplished pilot, to accompany me to Jack's class. The only condition was that he not critique any of my flight maneuvers from shore. Since he already had a seaplane rating, he elected to take the refresher course in the Maule seaplane. I signed up for the rating course in a two-person Piper Cub.

Day one dawned clear but unusually cool for South Florida in January. There was a gentle wind blowing, which I would later learn is a good thing when you fly off the water. Glassy water, when the air is dead still and the water surface looks like a mirror, is one of the most challenging conditions for a seaplane pilot. Since I hadn't flown a small airplane in a while and had never flown a Cub, I needed all the help I could get.

We arrived a half hour early at 7:00 a.m. The school is situated on the shore of Lake Jessie and is right next to Gilbert Airport, a small general aviation field with no control tower. Air-traffic control is done by eyeball, which can get sporty on a sunny weekend. The nearest radar is just north of the lake in a cop car chasing speeders down Route 92.

As you approach the building, it looks more like a quaint resort than a flight school. A small table, with chairs and a bright-green umbrella, occupies the deck in front of the building by the door, a suitable location for a picnic lunch.

A vintage ad for the Piper Cub hangs on the outside wall, with a cartoon bear cub holding a sign that says, "Fly for Fun CUB." The glass front door is obscured from top to bottom with a variety of decals applied by the various people who have flown there. They depict airlines, flying clubs, favorite airplanes, and aviation organizations.

Inside, we completed the paperwork, eager to explore the facility before ground school commenced.

We walked out to the end of the building, which extended over the water on stilts, to take in the view and see if we could spy some floatplanes in operation. There was a hanging two-person swing at the end of the dock, and the view from it was beautiful, with lake houses dotting the shoreline all around the perimeter.

The lake was empty, but to the left was a seaplane parked along the grassy beach with its floats nudged against the shore-line, secured by a rope attached to a tie-down loop anchored in the grass. To the right were two ramps used for launching the seaplanes. The water rippled slightly from the gentle wind out of the north as it lapped against the launching ramps in a soothing, hypnotic rhythm.

We stopped by the break room, which had the obligatory coffeepot with sugar and "dairy dust" creamer for the coffee. It was a little stale and watered down, not at all like Starbucks. However, if it had been Starbucks, it would've ruined the rustic vibe. It was the kind of coffee you expect at a seaplane base, something that tastes like you brewed it in the woods.

Several tables offered a view toward the western part of the lake and the two ramps, from where you could safely and smugly critique the arrivals and departures of other pilots.

We wandered into the empty briefing room and realized we were the only two students for the ground school that day. It was part briefing room, part pilot lounge. You got a sense of the passion the Browns and staff have for aviation from the artifacts and memorabilia scattered around.

A large folding table and chairs dominated the center of the room, and that's where our poor instructor would try to hammer home the fundamentals I had studied in my prework. On the table was a beaten red-and-white-plastic seaplane model, which was missing a few control surfaces, used with dramatic effect by the instructors to illustrate maneuvers and concepts. Behind it was a small whiteboard, and on the walls were photos of aircraft ranging from the tiny Cub to the hypersonic SR-71.

Yellowing emails taped to one wall identified the areas around the lake that were noise sensitive, which indicated the people who were most pissed off about the little Cubs buzzing low over their homes.

An article profiling the school from a back issue of AOPA's *Pilot Magazine* was framed prominently on the wall. There were also the odd airplane-for-sale flyers. An old plaid fabric sofa and coffee table anchored the back end of the room, a nod to the "lounge" function. The table was covered with out-of-date aviation magazines. In the corner above the sofa was suspended a model of a yellow Piper Cub, sans floats.

Eric Christensen, our ground instructor, wandered in right on time. He was a young man who was enthusiastic, articulate, and obviously spent a lot of time on the water. He would be Al's flight instructor and would later humble Al, who had been flying for 50 years, with his skill and proficiency on the water. I would be similarly humbled by my instructor.

He walked us through all the basics of floatplane flying, and like my Learjet ground school, it was a litany of the stupid, often fatal, mistakes seaplane pilots have made. If there are 100 ways to kill yourself in a light airplane, putting floats on it adds another 50. Hitting obstacles in the water, hitting trees, hitting boats, hitting other planes...the list is long but mainly involves hitting things.

In the course of two hours, the main rule I learned was to keep the nose of the airplane up or else the floats will dig into the water and flip you smartly onto your back, where you will float upside down underwater for a while. The procedure following such a mishap, which is hard to remember while you are submerged and suspended upside down, is to unbuckle your seat belt, open the airplane door, and swim your way to the surface before the whole contraption sinks to the bottom, taking you with it.

Needless to say, such a mishap is terrible because it is embarrassing, expensive, and potentially fatal, not necessarily in that order.

We took a break. Al went off with Eric, and I met my instructor, Ben Shipps. Ben was another young, experienced seaplane pilot, who'd spent a season in Alaska flying Beavers and

Cessna 206s in the bush. He was way overqualified to teach a land lover like me.

We exchanged pleasantries, and I learned that Ben, a husband and new father, had moved to Florida from Alaska. This job was much more conducive to family life than that of a bush pilot. We headed out to preflight the aircraft.

The Cub was a bright-yellow, high wing, two-seat aircraft mostly covered in fabric, with a tiny 100-HP engine, souped-up from the original 85. About 250 pounds of aluminum rigging, floats, and reinforcements turned it into a flying boat, which seemed a little out of place next to the delicate-looking fabric.

Ben walked me through a thorough preflight. There were two striking features. The first was the rigging for the rudders on the back of the floats, used to steer on the water at low speed, which looked like a spaghetti of stainless-steel cables and anchor points. The second was the engine, with exhaust stacks and cylinders that burst awkwardly from the side of the nose cowling and reminded me of the birth of that creature from the movie *Alien*. For somebody used to seeing a sleek jet engine nacelle, this just didn't seem right.

We gingerly got into the tandem aircraft, me first in the back, and then Ben in front. As Ben settled in, I had a somewhat disconcerting feeling. As I looked forward at the instrument panel, all I saw was the back of Ben's green-brown camo jacket. There were very few instruments on the panel to begin with, and now most of them were obscured by Ben. For someone used to the crutch of lots of instruments, this would be like flying with one eye closed. The only thing I could see was the engine RPM on the far left and the altimeter on the far right. The airspeed indicator was invisible.

"Hey, Ben, what do I do about airspeed?"

"Don't worry, we fly by feel and the pitch attitude of the nose versus the horizon," he replied.

This did not make me feel any better.

"Besides, the airspeed indicator isn't very accurate anyway."

That made me feel worse.

"Don't worry, you'll get the hang of it," he said cheerily.

Ben said, "Don't worry" to me a lot during those two days.

One pleasant surprise was the total lack of any type of two-way radio. I'd spent decades listening to endless demands from air traffic controllers on the radio. It was always, "turn right, slow down, descend, you turned the wrong way," followed invariably by, "Are you reading me okay?" It was pure heaven to learn that the only person I'd be listening to would be Ben, on the Cub's intercom headset.

Before we cranked up the engine, Ben explained one fundamental difference between land planes in seaplanes: once you start the engine, you can't stop a floatplane. It has only one gear, and that is Drive.

Obviously, this requires a bit of planning.

"We usually fly with the door open, but since it's cool, I think we'll close it," Ben said. That was fine with me because in every other airplane I've been in, having the door open in flight was a serious cause for concern.

Ben cranked up the engine, and we immediately began moving forward in the water, albeit slowly. He held the stick fully back to keep the floats from digging in. Unfortunately, this kept the nose up and made it impossible to see where we were going, despite how I craned my neck. Ben made small right and left turns to clear the area in front of us.

"Why don't you take control," Ben said. "Just make sure you hold the stick full back to keep the nose up." I imagined instantly burying the nose of the floats into the water and flipping over like a bad surfer at Mavericks. With my hand tight on the stick, the blood squeezed from my fingertips from my death grip, I managed to keep the nose elevated.

We S-turned our way to the downwind side of the lake, but I felt like I was sitting in a big hole of water.

Then came my favorite part of floatplane training: turning into the wind. Why? Because you don't have to do anything. The airplane turns into the wind on its own, like a weathervane rooster on top of a barn.

"I'll make the first takeoff. Just follow me through on the controls." We ran the shortest before-takeoff checklist I've ever seen, which included only four items.

"Here we go." Ben held the stick back and applied full throttle, and we lugubriously dragged through the water, slowly gaining speed. Suddenly, the nose popped up even more to an impossible angle, then Ben released some of the back pressure on the stick, and we were out of the water hole pretty much level, like a boat on the step. Finally, I could almost see over the nose.

We lifted off, and once free of the drag of the water, climbed gently over Gilbert Field.

Even with the door closed, the little Cub was extraordinarily drafty. Large gaps between the door, windows, and frame allowed air to blow noisily into the cockpit, and I was glad I'd worn a jacket. You could feel every puff of wind, every thermal. I was used to big airplanes where every molecule of air was compressed, filtered, warmed, or cooled appropriately, and metered into the cabin. The Cub felt like three blow-dryers, all set to cold, were randomly sweeping over me.

We leveled off at the ridiculously low altitude of 500 feet. Previously, 500 feet was an altitude I occupied for but a split second while taking off or landing.

"Sixty miles per hour is the magic number," Ben said. "Climb at 60, cruise at 60, approach at 60."

"Like I said, Ben, I can't see the airspeed indicator," I pleaded.

"Don't worry." There it was again. Ben was awful damned optimistic. Obviously, his bubble of comfort was a lot bigger than mine.

We did a few maneuvers to get the feel of the airplane. Ben was right. After a while I didn't need the airspeed indicator to tell my speed. It was all pitch attitude and feel.

We wasted no time getting to takeoffs and landings. And there were lots of different kinds: normal, crosswind, rough water, confined space, and the mother of all seaplane landings, the dreaded glassy water landing.

Glassy water landings are challenging because when the air is dead calm, the surface of the water is so smooth and reflective that the pilot has zero depth perception. The solution to this is to set yourself up over a flat shoreline and get down to a very low altitude over the shore, where you have some depth perception. You raise the nose and add some power *before* you cross over the water, and then—wait. You hold that nose-high attitude, gently descending, dum-dee-dum, for what seems like forever, and wait until you touch down. This procedure keeps the nose up, which in turn prevents the floats from digging in and. . . well, you know the rest.

I now understood this concept, so we practiced a few of these on nonglassy water, but in my heart of hearts, I really didn't believe what Eric and Ben had told me. Come on, how hard could it be?

The next day I found out.

The morning dawned cool and still, with not a ripple on the lake. We flew north to one of the many other lakes in the area, spreading our noise around so as not to generate any new complaints.

I set up for the glassy water landing as we had practiced the day before. Everything seemed just hunky dory. We found a flat shoreline, planned for a nice long final approach, and at about 50 feet, I raised the pitch, inched in a little power, and we crossed the shoreline.

Once over the water, it looked like we had just flown into a fog bank. You couldn't see anything. No depth perception, no reference. The water and sky were one. I guess Eric and Ben weren't full of it after all! It was very disorienting, but I held the attitude for a long time, and magically we touched down, nose high.

We banged around the lakes for another hour, practicing all the maneuvers for the check ride, over and over until Ben deemed me ready.

I've taken hundreds of phase checks, oral exams, written exams, and practical tests in my years of flying. Even though I have never failed one, I'm still nervous before each. The fact that I've never failed puts even more pressure on me to avoid this one being the first. I wondered: Why the heck did I put myself in this position, anyway? I didn't have to take this course. Hell, after today, I may never fly a seaplane again.

Jon Brown, the examiner, was cordial and relaxed. He gave me a thorough oral exam. We jumped in the airplane, and in less than an hour, I was done. I was now a single-engine sea pilot. Phew.

In these two days, I conducted 46 takeoffs and landings, more than I'd do in six months as an airline pilot. I flew by the seat of my pants, but I expanded my knowledge of flying. More importantly, I blew my bubble of comfort up so big you could fly it to Oz and back. You'll never know what you are capable of until you try.

CHAPTER 19

GET TO THE POINT

I know that you believe you understand what you think I said,

but I'm not sure that you realize

that what you heard was not what I meant.

—Robert McCloskey

If you have kids, have been a kid, or have listened to a kid, you understand the importance of clear communication. It's one of our most valuable skills in life. I learned early on how important it was—not only to read between the lines but also to get my lines right.

Back when I was 17 years old, after my harrowing flight where I scared Eddie, I called my dad to tell him about it.

I started by talking about how I convinced Eddie to go, our drive to the airport, getting the parachute, including every detail. Dad interrupted me.

"Today, my patient Ethel Johnson came into my office with a cut on her finger. I said, 'Mrs. Johnson, how did you cut your finger?'"

"She said, 'Well, Dr. Forte, I got up a little late today and had my usual breakfast of oatmeal with a little brown sugar on it and a cup of green tea. Then I got dressed and put on a skirt but realized it was a bit chilly, so I switched to pants.'

"She went on. 'I got in my car and put the key in the ignition, but wouldn't you know it. I had the wrong keys. I got out, went inside, and got the right keys. I started the car and backed out of the driveway but saw the newspaper lying there, so I stopped, got out, and picked up the paper and put it in the car.'"

"It took her 15 minutes to tell me she cut her finger on a cart at the grocery store," Dad said.

I was starting to get *his* point that I should just get to *the* point.

"Dad, I fell out of a roll, did a split S when going too fast, and pulled four Gs," I said.

"That's more like it, Steve," he said. There was a pause, and then he said incredulously, "Four Gs?"

There's nothing more annoying and potentially disastrous than poor communication. Life is full of bad results that can be tied directly to people not communicating in a prompt, clear, concise way, especially in aviation. The worst aviation disaster ever, the collision of two B747s on the ground in Tenerife, Canary Islands, was caused mainly by poor communications.

While that is an extreme consequence of poor communication, many examples show just how important it is to communicate effectively.

Gary Meermans, the chief pilot for United Airlines in Los Angeles for many years, was a master of subtle but effective communication. Soft-spoken and avuncular, he was widely respected by the pilots and the union and could fly the hell out of an airplane.

One day he was piloting a B767 with a somewhat disgruntled first officer who we will call Mark. He had been a first officer for a long time, stuck in that seat due to a lack of growth at the airline due to a recession and his refusal to move to a more junior pilot base. He was tall and thin with reddish hair and freckles, with an annoying nasal tone to his voice.

As they leveled off at cruise, Julie, the lead flight attendant, entered the cockpit.

"You guys ready to eat?" she said.

"Sure," Gary said. "Whaddaya got back there?"

"Well, as usual, I have chicken and beef. No surprises," Julie said.

"Mark, you first," said Gary.

Mark said, "Neither one. I ordered a special meal, the chef salad. Do you have my chef salad? That's all I ever eat on the airplane, the chef salad."

"Hmm, I didn't see it back there, but I'll look again. It might be in the aft galley. How about you, Gary?" Julie said.

"I'll take the chicken, thanks, whenever you get a chance. With a black coffee, please."

She left and returned a few minutes later with one meal.

"Here you go, Gary. I'm sorry, Mark, but I searched the galleys and couldn't find your special meal. I guess they didn't board it. How about I take the salads off a couple of coach meals and combine them into one big one for you?"

Mark exhaled loudly. "No. I ordered the chef salad, and that's what I want. If I can't have my chef salad, I don't want anything." He folded his arms in defiance.

"Okay, suit yourself, but let me know if you change your mind," Julie said, and she left the cockpit.

Gary dug into his lunch. "Rubber chicken, gotta love it!"

Mark remained sullen, shoulders slumped, staring straight ahead at the instrument panel.

After a few minutes, Gary finally spoke up. "Hey, what's the deal with the chef salad?"

Mark loosened his seat belt so he could turn in his seat to face Gary squarely. "You know what just happened, right?"

Gary looked perplexed. "Yeah, the dipshits in the kitchen didn't board your meal."

"No, no, no. That's not what happened. Here's what happened. I order my chef salad. They board my chef salad. The flight attendants *see* my chef salad, and it looks good. Then one of the flight attendants *steals* my chef salad and eats it. Then they tell me, 'Oh, the kitchen forgot to board it.' Happens all the time. I'm so sick of it. That is *my* chef salad," Mark said.

Gary stopped chewing in amazement, barely able to keep the rubber chicken in his mouth.

Mark continued. "I am never eating another thing on board an airplane unless it is my chef salad. I AM GOING TO TEACH THESE FLIGHT ATTENDANTS A LESSON!"

Gary swallowed, paused for a moment, and asked: "How much longer do you think they can *take* it?"

Sometimes behavior can affect good communication. One captain who was a demanding jerk refused any input from his first officers—or any crewmember, for that matter. It got so bad that the first officer simply stopped offering suggestions at all, a dangerous situation.

As the captain lined up to the runway to land, the first officer noticed they were aimed at the wrong airport. Since his input has been ignored each time before, he decided to stay silent again.

They touched down safely, turned off the runway, and then the captain realized his mistake.

"Tell them we landed at the wrong airport," he said glumly.

The first officer said, "I did that five minutes ago when we were on final approach." He was so demoralized that he allowed the captain to make a serious error.

In another incident, the crew of a wide body DC-10 jet was pulling into a very tight parking space, with a large light pole on the right. The captain couldn't see it from where he was seated, so he relied on his first officer on the right side to guide him.

"Come ahead. We are good," the first officer said.

The captain slowed his taxi to a crawl. "We okay?"

"We are still good. Come on, come on," the first officer said. "We're good. Keep it coming."

The captain continued forward, trusting his fellow crewmember. Suddenly, they felt a jolt as the right wing struck the pole.

"Oh my God, *you* just hit the light pole!" said the first officer.

What was obviously a severe communication breakdown between colleagues quickly turned into a solo project, with the first officer assuming none of the blame when push came to shove.

Miscommunication happens outside of the cockpit, too. And occasionally it's hard to tell whether a person is being serious or just messing with you.

When fuel prices spiked, most airlines put into place a policy of boarding only enough fuel to fly the trip safely. Why? Because the more fuel you have onboard, the heavier the airplane is, and you will burn more fuel just to carry the weight of the extra fuel.

However, in the real world, unforeseen things happen. Airports close unexpectedly, winds are less favorable than planned, and the weather turns out worse than forecast, which makes pilots exceptionally skeptical and cautious. They also know one thing for sure: you can make a lot of mistakes and still be okay, but if you run out of fuel, the flight will probably not end well. Hence, a lot of pilots like to add fuel for such contingencies, even though it means you might burn a little more in total.

To explain the new "Fly with less fuel" campaign, one management pilot was camped out in the operations area where pilots planned their flights. One grizzled old-school captain was looking at his flight plan and told the clerk, "Gimme another 5,000 pounds of fuel."

The management pilot heard this, wandered over to the planning counter, and engaged the old captain in conversation.

"Do you know that you will burn 1,000 pounds of additional fuel just to carry around that extra 5,000 pounds?" he said.

Instead of reconsidering his decision and adding less fuel (or none at all), the captain turned to the clerk and said, "Make that 6,000 pounds."

The entire lounge burst out in laughter.

It's also important to be careful with jargon.

I was riding on an airliner as a passenger in the back row. The pilot got on the PA and said, "Well folks, the weather in Denver is 400 broken and two," meaning a 400-foot cloud base and two miles' visibility.

The nervous flyer next to me bolted upright in his seat with panic in his eyes and said, "If there is something broken in two, then I'm getting off!"

There can also be unintended consequences when communication goes out that others find insulting.

One airline manager was incensed that pilots were walking around O'Hare airport in their uniforms in the summer, licking ice cream cones. So he put out a memo telling pilots that the practice was "not professional." You can imagine the result. The next day every pilot was eating an ice cream cone. Pilots who didn't like ice cream, pilots who were lactose intolerant—all licking ice cream cones.

False assumptions can also feed miscommunication.

One afternoon a woman pilot friend of mine was in the ladies' room at the airport in full uniform. She'd just eaten lunch and was brushing her teeth. A woman came up to her out of nowhere and said, "My sister would be so proud of you!"

She said, "Oh, is your sister a pilot?"

The woman said, "No, she's a *dentist.*"

It's also a good idea to be succinct in written correspondence. Mark Twain once said, "I didn't have time to write a short letter, so I wrote a long one instead." It is hard to write tight.

I once worked with a pilot, Rich Moran, who was a serial letter writer. When you had to type a letter on paper, it was a natural deterrent to wandering missives. Unfortunately, email made it a lot easier for people like Rich to send long diatribes. Email fed his letter-writing habit like pot feeds the munchies. No matter where he flew or what he did, a lengthy email followed. To make matters worse, he appeared to have no desire or capacity to read what he wrote before he sent it. A simple email that intended to say, "We need to do a better job boarding earlier," would read, "We ned ta due a bedder jib boaring oilier."

Colleagues of mine began to emulate his style just to bug me. One of my guys asked for a day off as follows: "Stive, kin I toke Mundy iff?"

And if you answered Rich's email, another one would follow, 100 percent of the time. It was like the classic video game Pong, where the little ball always came back. We gave him the nickname "Rich Moremail" because no matter what we replied, there would be more email to follow.

Finally, I had a master stroke. I began to reply, "Call me."
He never did.

No one can read your mind, nor can you read theirs, however intuitive you think you may be. Clear communication is essential to explain, to empathize and innovate, to build teams, and to earn trust. Even when it's uncomfortable, have the conversation, ask the question, and build the bridge.

CHAPTER 20

JEFF BEZOS WAS WRONG?

All technology should be assumed guilty until proven innocent.

—David Brower

Humans are amazing, complicated, wondrous, and often fallible. Although I wouldn't suggest that you tell your boss he or she is off base, remember that even the smartest people in the world can be wrong. Sometimes logic fails when people are swayed by their perceptions, prejudices, or past experiences.

These days, everyone from the *Harvard Business Journal* to Jeff Bezos is prognosticating about how technology, of some form or another, will replace us all. While I think that makes for a sensational headline, I don't believe the human race is quite dead yet. I think we still have a long way to go, as does my friend Ginger, also an ai rline pilot. One evening a few years ago, Ginger took on an influential business leader to prove just that point.

Passionate about women's rights, Ginger is a senior captain at a big airline who has suffered for decades working as a woman in a man's world. These experiences have made her tough, and she can stand up to anyone, anywhere, anytime.

One of the great frustrations of her career is that when she got hired over 30 years ago, women made up 5 percent of the airline pilot population. Today, it is only 7 percent, which is dismal progress.

Ginger also finds it ironic that when you go back to the World War II era, woman pilots weren't allowed into combat, where they *might* get shot at. However, they were permitted to tow training targets stateside, which *guaranteed* they would get shot at.

It doesn't help the cause of equality in the cockpit when you watch movies and TV. I'm sure Ian Fleming thought it was quite progressive to show character Pussy Galore (don't get Ginger started on that) in command of the title character's private jet in the 1964 James Bond movie *Goldfinger*. And it was even more astounding that Ms. Galore was assisted by a woman first officer. When you zoom in on her, you will note that she is reading something. No, she was not paging through an aircraft technical manual or reading an aeronautical chart. She was flipping through a fashion magazine.

Mattel got it partly right. It designed a doll called Pilot Barbie to inspire young girls. At least Mattel put her in pants so she could navigate the control yoke. That said, when you look at the uniform, she just looks like a flight attendant wearing a hat.

After almost a century of women piloting some of the largest and most complex airplanes in the air, flying upside down inches from the ground at air shows, bombing the bejesus out of terrorists, rocketing into space, and often flying circles around their male counterparts, they still make up only a tiny fraction of the airline pilot population. Pilots like Ginger have done their best to improve those bleak stats by encouraging young people, especially women, to pursue careers in aviation.

It's no surprise then that anyone who opposed that mission, no matter how influential, would incur her wrath. A not-so-subtle example of this occurred at the Annual Pathfinder Awards

Dinner at the Boeing Museum of Flight in Seattle. The award honors individuals with ties to the Pacific Northwest who have made significant contributions to the development of the aerospace industry. The Pathfinder Award honorees are selected by the Museum of Flight Board of Trustees, and this year, Jeff Bezos was one of them.

In case you have been totally unconscious for the past 20 years, or have never made an online purchase of a book, shirt, computer, printer, Kindle, bathroom scale, Brita water filter, or any of a million other things, Jeff Bezos made much of that possible. He is one of the smartest and most successful businessmen and entrepreneurs ever. Founder and CEO of Seattle-based Amazon, he pretty much revolutionized e-commerce. His net worth places him as the richest man in the world. He's also the founder of Blue Origin and Bezos Expeditions and has a long-standing passion for space exploration, including low-cost reusable space flight technology.

When I arrived for the event, the museum was slowly filling to capacity. It was a very diverse crowd of pilots, educators, engineers, entrepreneurs, and students, united by their love of aviation.

Cocktail bars were scattered among the roughly 150 different aircraft and spacecraft in and around the museum. I saw Ginger there, and we each grabbed a wine and immediately noticed several administrators from the University of North Dakota (UND), her alma mater. UND has a phenomenal aviation program, although there is little to do in Grand Forks other than fly, go to class, and avoid frostbite. In other words, it's a great place to make learning to fly your priority.

At that point we noticed Bezos standing off to the side, talking to a few high school students. No entourage, no apparent bodyguard, just chatting with some of the attendees. Like almost everyone else, he was wearing formal attire with a white aviation scarf around his neck, as is the tradition at this event.

We politely waited for our turn to speak with him, and when it came, Ginger introduced herself and told him she was an airline pilot.

"That's great," he said, "because only about 7 percent of airline pilots in the United States are women."

She was surprised he knew that statistic, and he seemed impressed that she had become successful in such a male-dominated field. Ginger thanked him for talking to students at Aviation High School, which is affiliated with the museum, and for encouraging them to pursue aviation as well as STEM subjects (science, technology, engineering, and math).

We yielded to others who wanted to talk to him and returned to the UND contingent. "I just talked to Jeff Bezos. What an interesting and unassuming man," Ginger said to Beth Bjerke, associate dean and professor of aviation at UND.

"Obviously, he didn't tell you what he said to the students at Aviation High School yesterday," Beth said.

"What?" Ginger asked.

"He told them not to pursue a career as a pilot because that job will be obsolete in 10 years, replaced by robots."

"You have to be (expletive) kidding me," Ginger said, confounded. "I'll be right back."

Anyone who knows Ginger will tell you that you do not want to get between her and her objective. Throwing courtesy aside, she weaved her way through the thickening crowd like a hockey forward on a power play and slid in front of Bezos.

"Remember me?" she said. "Did you seriously tell a group of high school students who wanted to become pilots not to pursue it?"

"Well, yes. You see, Ginger, you don't realize you are flying in the Golden Age of Aviation."

"I thought Howard Hughes flew in the Golden Age of Aviation," she replied.

"You have 10 years to go, and you should be okay, but after 10 years we will all be flying around in unmanned airplanes," Bezos said.

Much to Ginger's chagrin, he correctly pegged her age. He also knew off the top of his head that the mandatory retirement age for an airline pilot in the United States is 65. We knew the guy was smart, but the breadth of his aviation knowledge was surprising.

"I respectfully disagree and don't deny that the technology to do that is already here. But even if you can do it, do you really think people would happily get on an airliner knowing nothing was flying the plane except a computer? That would be a tough sell," she said. "You are going to need someone up there to turn everything off when some 13-year-old kid hacks into the computer and tries to crash the plane."

"Ginger, it's not good to lean against technology," he said, smiling.

"I'm going to trade in my wine for a martini," she said, and they parted ways.

Now I'm a big fan of technology, but you must be practical about it. Seventy-five years ago, some people wouldn't get on an elevator unless there was an elevator operator on board. Shuttle trains at airports had a conductor, and amusement park rides had people operating them, but that's all changed. I'll command my own elevator and ride in a conductor-less train. I'll even get on the unmanned El Diablo roller coaster at Six Flags, which spins you around like blood plasma in a centrifuge, then jerks you left and right like a crocodile swallowing a badger. But here's the big difference. An elevator goes up and down, a train goes left and right, and even a roller coaster speeds along a well-defined track. But an airplane, with its almost infinite number of possible movements, hundreds of things that can go wrong, and errant passengers and unpredictable weather, is an entirely different thing. Those are a lot of variables to crunch, even for IBM's Watson, so it's going to be a long time before people trust that technology.

I sat at the dinner that night in the shadow of an SR-71 spy plane and listened to Jeff Bezos talk about his management principles. He said that you don't choose your passions; they choose you. That you need to be stubborn on vision but flexible on the details. And that failure and invention are inseparable twins.

"If you know something is going to work, then it's not an experiment," he said.

But the thing that really struck me was when he said good leaders "are right a lot." Although that sounds pretty simple, he went on to say that with practice, you can develop this skill by listening well, changing your mind when the facts change, reconsidering the facts over time, and being willing to disconfirm your own convictions.

He didn't change his mind that night, but based on what he said about being flexible—and if pilots like my friend have anything to say about it—I'm pretty sure he will. However capable machines may become, they will never replace our essential humanity. That's our ace in the hole.

CHAPTER 21

ENJOY YOUR RIDE

Forever is composed of nows.

—Emily Dickinson

As you probably figured out from the previous chapters, one secret to success is to focus on things you can control. Another is that if you seize the unique opportunities that come your way, you can reach your goals. You can use all 20 of my other secrets in this book or just those that make sense for you. It is your career to manage.

I will share one last secret.

You don't have to bring your best game all the time. It's impossible to go 100 percent every minute of the day. You can be successful in life while operating at a moderate pace most of the time. You just need to recognize when you are at one of those inflection points, where you must bring it all and apply yourself when it counts.

Whether it's flying an F-16 through mountain canyons, formation flying with a B747, pulling out of a poorly executed split S, or safely landing a powerless jet on the Hudson, you need to bring that intensity at the right time. And when you add up the minutes of your life, there are relatively few pivotal moments where you must perform with flawless intensity to succeed.

I've had many role models, some of them good and some of them bad. Even so, the most important thing I've learned from them all is to find something you are passionate about, and I was fortunate to discover my passion at a young age. If you are going to spend one-third of your life working, you better find a vocation you enjoy.

Whether I was drilling ladders at Safe-T, sweating on the ramp at Cochise Airlines, or jumping out of an airplane with a vampire, it was all with a greater plan in mind. Every move I made brought me closer to my ultimate goal even though much of it was challenging. Forever may as well be now. What are you waiting for?

What People Are Saying about

TAKE OFF! 21 High-Flying Secrets for Career Success

"This is a source of sound practical business advice and tips for success, whether you are a new graduate, career changer or seasoned professional. Steve captures the essence of Virgin America's innovation and genius and illustrates why learning from those who are at the top of their game is a winning strategy."
—David Cush, former CEO, Virgin America Airlines

"From his humble beginnings in operations to his various leadership roles throughout the airline industry, Captain Forte shares his range of experience to help you craft a flight plan for success in both life and business. TAKE OFF is a must read!"
—Andrew P. Studdert, former chief operating officer, United Airlines

"In TAKE OFF!, Steve Forte shares valuable lessons he's learned through personal experience and observing excellence in others. Whether pulling Gs in an F-16 fighter or watching the remarkable teamwork of the flight deck crew launching jets from an aircraft carrier, Steve distills the essence of the people who make the extraordinary an everyday occurrence."
—Rear Admiral Mark H. Buzby, USN (retired)

"Having known Steve professionally for over 20 years, it's no surprise that he has created TAKE OFF! to share what he has learned from other successful people. Each chapter delivers a most interesting, sometimes funny, and always relevant lesson. The result is a book that generates thought and introspection and provides a straightforward path down your road to success.

—Captain Rob Giguere, retired EVP Operations, Air Canada

"Steve Forte is a pilot I trust. It turns out he's a reliable narrator, too. I enjoyed reading this tale of a bottom-entry bum learning his way through serendipitous lessons. It is wisdom disguised as common sense, and a clean read to boot. I'd say it's an enriching tale to anyone who wants a peek behind the curtain of the airline industry."

—Matt Walsh, actor on the HBO comedy *VEEP*, founding member of the Upright Citizens Brigade.

ABOUT THE AUTHOR

Stephen A. Forte is a pilot, aviation executive, entrepreneur, author, speaker, educator, movie producer, and aviation consultant. He started his career at United Airlines flying regularly scheduled flights, eventually transitioning to various management roles, ultimately becoming the senior vice president of Flight Operations and director of Operations, responsible for all aspects of United's worldwide flight operations. Forte helped lead the airline through many challenges, including the terrorist attacks on 9/11.

He later served as CEO of aviation tech start-up Naverus, Inc. and chief operating officer for Virgin America Airlines until it was acquired by Alaska Air Group. He has flown over 50 airplane models to almost every corner of the world and is currently vice president of training for a major airline.

Forte's expertise goes beyond aviation. He is executive producer of the movie *Under the Eiffel Tower*, starring Matt Walsh and Judith Godreche. A frequent speaker, Forte has addressed a variety of industry groups and given motivational speeches at colleges and universities.

LAUNCH YOUR CAREER TO THRILLING NEW HEIGHTS

Dear friend,

To help make your career journey easier, faster, and more successful than you ever dreamed, I've assembled *three* **powerful success and career tools** as my gift to you for reading my book. All 100 percent free.

1. Get instant access to my breakthrough reports: "8 Secrets to Planning Your Path for Career Success," and "Managing Up—How to Support Your Boss and Get the Credit Your Deserve." You'll use these powerful strategies for the rest of your career.

2. I've uploaded a bonus chapter to my book to give you specific, street-smart tactics for getting to the next level.

3. Get priority notification of new cutting-edge articles about specific strategies for accelerating your career path forward.

Simply leave your primary email address at:
HighFlyingSuccessSecrets.com, and I'll take it from there.

Best wishes for your success.
Steve

CPSIA information can be obtained
at www.ICGtesting.com
Printed in the USA
LVHW041211190819
628119LV00003B/133/P